A man from Danville who lost his eyesight in an accident is asked what he misses seeing the most. "Springtime," he says. "April on Mount Diablo. But you know," he adds with a bit of a smile, "I still go up there. It smells heavenly."

LARRY ULRICH

A father and son are fishing on the shore of Lake Oroville. It's been three hours and not a bite. Over a million fish have been planted in this lake, the father thinks to himself, Where are they? Maybe it's the wrong time of day or the wrong lure. Suddenly a bite. A big bite on the father's line, and he hands the rod and reel to his son. "Easy," the father says, praying the fish won't get away. "Eeeeeasy does it." Ten minutes later the ecstatic boy hauls in a rainbow trout.

JEFF GNASS

CALIFORNIA

State

Parks

NUMBER TWO

KIM HEACOX

FALCON PRESS PUBLISHING CO. INC.

JAMES M. HARRIS

A young man who left the Soviet Union during the Stalinist purges of the late thirties is an old man now living in San Francisco. He loves America, but in the deep recesses of his mind he misses his motherland. Those childhood memories die hard. On Memorial Day he drives north from San Francisco to attend Russian Orthodox services at Fort Ross State Historic Park. He takes a deep breath and proudly enters the small chapel he helped to rebuild after a disastrous fire. Standing there in the salty California air on soil once claimed by Russians, he smiles and feels good. Both his homes are under his feet.

It's January at Año Nuevo State Reserve. Two bull elephant seals meet on the beach at the border separating their harems. With backs arched and heads raised, they glare at each other. Each is 16 feet long and weighs 4,000 pounds. The surrounding smaller seals scatter away. First one bull trumpets, then the other. Had one been able to trumpet louder it might have intimidated its adversary into retreat. But this is an even match. These two patriarchs are in their prime—both 8 to 10 years old, both battle-tested but not crippled, both determined to mate with as many female elephant seals as possible.

They charge. The battle lasts ten minutes, but to the people watching from behind a nearby beach berm, it seems like an eternity. The bulls tear and growl at each other, drawing blood but inflicting no serious damage. Finally, one overpowers the other. For one long moment the people stand silent and still.

Someone finally exhales and says, "I've never seen anything like that before."

A journalist in the back is still writing; he feels like a war correspondent. Six weeks later a young girl from the group wins a science award at her school. The title of her winning report: "Elephants on the Beach."

FRANK S. BALTHIS

California Geographic Series Staff

Publishers: Michael S. Sample, Bill Schneider
Editor: Marnie Hagmann
Photo editors: Michael S. Sample, Bill Schneider, Jeri Walton
Design: DD Dowden
Graphics: DD Dowden
Marketing Director: Kelly Simmons

Front cover photo

Tree lupines on headlands above Stump Beach Cove, Salt Point State Park, California; photo by Larry Ulrich.

Back cover photos

Clockwise from top: California redwoods and azaleas at Big Basin Redwoods State Park; photo by Ed Cooper. Angel Island State Park; photo by Frank S. Balthis. Joshua trees and the San Gabriel Mountains seen from Saddleback Butte State Park; photo by Ed Cooper.

Copyright © 1987 by Falcon Press Publishing Co., Inc., Helena and Billings, Montana.

Published in cooperation with the California Department of Parks and Recreation.

Library of Congress Number: 86-82748
ISBN: 0-937959-07-3 (softcover)
ISBN: 0-937959-08-1 (hardcover)

Design, typesetting, and other prepress work by Falcon Press, Helena, Montana.

Printed in Hong Kong.

The author

Kim Heacox migrates between California and Alaska with his wife, Melanie, a park ranger. He has written for *Audubon*, *National Wildlife*, and National Geographic *Traveler* magazines, and he regularly contributes human interest stories to the National Geographic News Service and writes on public land issues for the Los Angeles Times-Washington Post News Service. Between writing assignments, he abandons his computer for a camera and disappears into the mountains.

A dedication

To Patty Brown and Evan Jones-Toscano, dedicated rangers.

D. CAVAGNARO

A boy born and raised in Oakland visits Henry W. Coe State Park. It's his first time out in the country, and he wants to know who put all the dirt on the road.

Acknowledgments

The idea of this book began years ago during a taco dinner in Anza-Borrego Desert State Park with photographers Larry and Donna Ulrich. The California Geographic Series had not yet been born, but when it was, and when Bill Schneider, publisher of Falcon Press asked Larry and Donna about an author for *California State Parks,* they recommended me. I thank them deeply, and I thank Bill for putting his faith in a writer he had never met or heard of.

In many respects the making of this book parallels the making of a park itself. It takes vision, cooperation, and hard work, and these people excel at them all. A heartfelt thanks to Marnie Hagmann, my editor, for her skill and sensitivity, and to DD Dowden for her imagination and patience. With the California Department of Parks and Recreation in Sacramento, Randy Jamison and Barbara Rathbun provided important resources and encouragement. And to Joe Engbeck, Jr., a California scholar and writer of tremendous caliber, my appreciation for valuable corrections to the manuscript.

To others within or related to the California State Park System who volunteered their time and resources, I salute you: Bud Getty, Frank Balthis, Mark C. Jorgensen, Ken McKowen, Donna Gillette, Roger McKasson, Jose Ignacio Rivera, Betsy Knaak, and Dorothy Lyons. A special nod to Mike Bishop and Edward H. Waldheim of the Off-Highway Motor Vehicle Recreation Commission, whose help and expertise proved immensely valuable.

To good friends Clark and Maureen Brink, thanks for the fresh vegetables and the floor space. And to Stan, Gretchen, and Erin Carrick, thanks for the undying support and interest. And lastly, to Melanie, a loving wife and good friend (and a darn good editor, too), my deepest, sincerest gratitude.

DAVID MUENCH

A successful lobbyist for a national conservation organization is interviewed by a newspaper reporter on Capitol Hill in Washington, D.C.

"How did you become interested in the environment?" the reporter asks.

"I grew up in California and my parents always took me to beautiful parks and wildlife reserves."

"You mean Yosemite and Sequoia?"

"Well, we went there, but my favorite was Point Lobos."

"Oh," the reporter says, obviously unimpressed. "Is that in Mexico?"

Contents

PAUL R. JOHNSON

A teenage boy recognizes the man standing in line in front of him in a San Diego supermarket. The face is familiar but not the place.

"Don't I know you?" he asks.

The man is a ranger from nearby Ocotillo Wells State Vehicular Recreation Area. A year earlier the boy had tumbled from his off-road vehicle head first down a deep ravine there. He had broken his back and had a floating bone chip near his spinal cord; a wrong move could have paralyzed him. When help arrived he was starting to convulse.

The ranger checked the boy's vital signs and for two hours—until a medical evacuation helicopter arrived—immobilized the boy by holding his head between his knees and pinning his shoulders down with his arms. It was a long evening. A week later he visited the boy in the hospital and was pleased to find that the prognosis for a full recovery was excellent. It was from that visit that the boy rekindled his fuzzy remembrance of the ranger's face.

Now, standing outside the supermarket, the boy takes the opportunity to say thank you. They exchange addresses, shake hands, and promise to keep in touch.

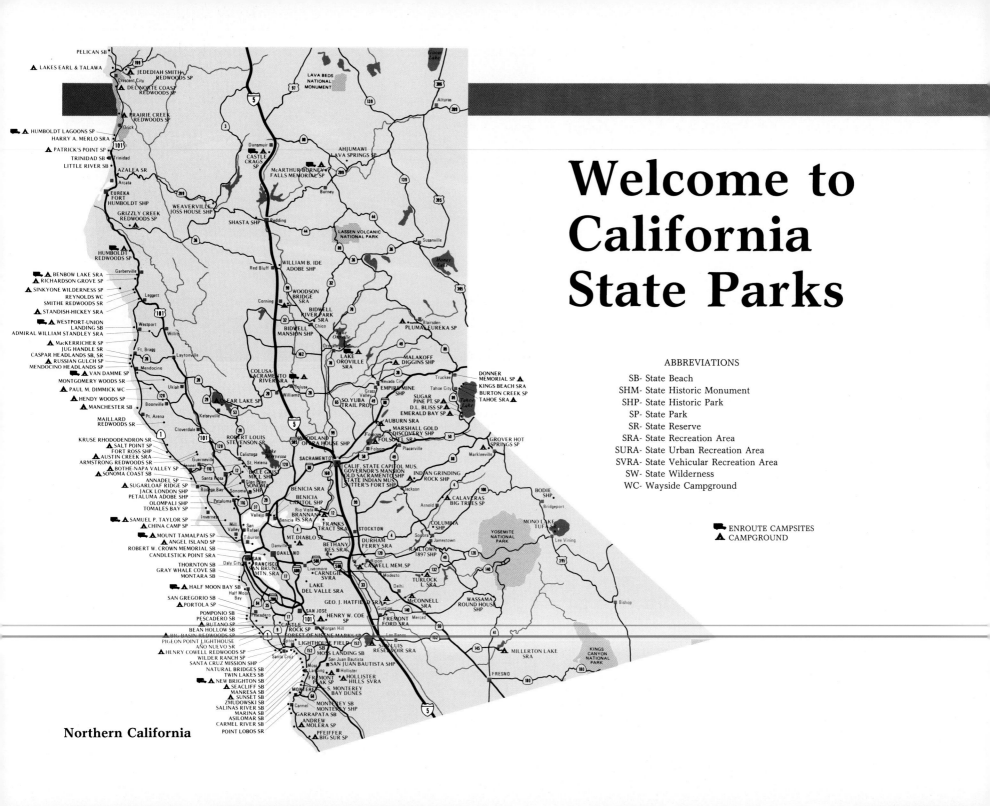

Welcome to California State Parks

ABBREVIATIONS

SB- State Beach
SHM- State Historic Monument
SHP- State Historic Park
SP- State Park
SR- State Reserve
SRA- State Recreation Area
SURA- State Urban Recreation Area
SVRA- State Vehicular Recreation Area
SW- State Wilderness
WC- Wayside Campground

ENROUTE CAMPSITES
▲ CAMPGROUND

Northern California

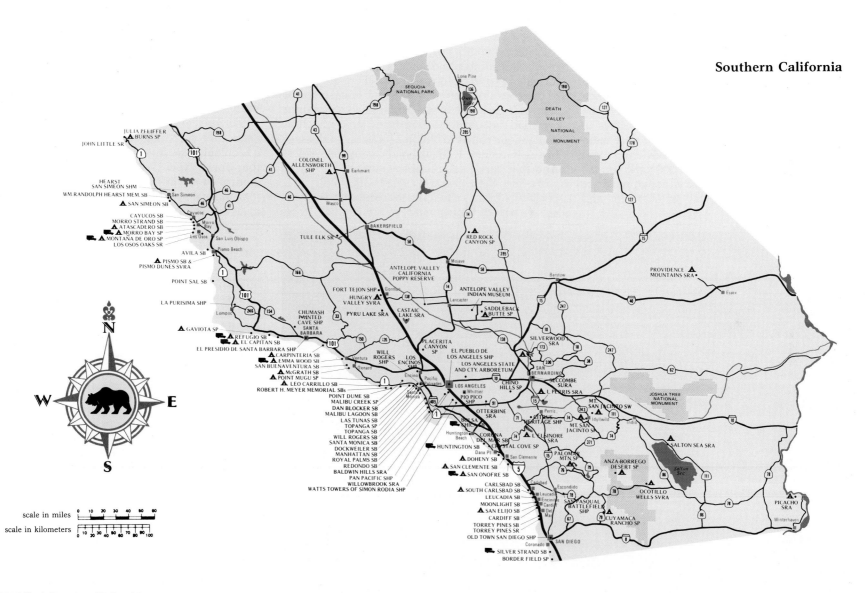

Southern California

© 1985 California Department of Parks and Recreation
Map courtesy California Department of Parks and
Recreation. Map design and layout, Alex Eng.

Introduction

Here is California in all her diversity, complexity, and beauty, polished like a pearl in a state park system many people consider the finest in the nation. A high school teacher in Los Angeles once remarked that if she could give her students the best education and recreation California has to offer, she'd load them into a bus and take them to every state park, reserve, beach, wilderness, and recreation area. There are about 300 park "units" totaling one million acres, and although most are small in size, they stand tall in character and importance.

Protected within are some of California's rarest plants and animals and some of its finest archaeological sites and historical areas. There are places to discover, to learn, and to enjoy. A calendar of statewide park events lists dozens of activities from crawdad days, banana slug races, polo matches, and antique shows to old-time jubilees, wildflower hikes, luminaria festivals, and steam train rides. And that barely scratches the surface.

We need these parks. We need wild country and pockets of history and room for recreation as much as we need timber and minerals and good vegetables. We need places that remind us of who we are and where we came from. "Something will have gone out of us as a people if we ever let the remaining wilderness be destroyed," writes Wallace Stegner. "Without any remaining wilderness we are committed wholly, without chance for even momentary reflection and rest, to a headlong drive into our technological termite-life, the Brave New World of a completely man-controlled environment."

California's state parks offer us that reflection and rest. They offer us endless, priceless opportunities to take a deep breath and to get away from it all.

California's population doubled in the last 30 years, and visitation to her state parks jumped 1,000 percent. But acreage in the park system increased only 60 percent. This math adds up to problems. In a democracy of the people, by the people, and for the people, it becomes you and I, the very ones who create parks, who can destroy parks. We have innocent tendencies of loving them to death.

One of the most conspicuous residents on the forest floor, a redwood sorrel (Oxalis oregana), left, brightens the green world of the coast with its pink-lavender blossoms, rewarding those who look down as well as up. Spring is the best time of year to see these flowers and others of the redwood groves. JEFF FOOTT

The small, elegant Carmel River runs out of the coast mountains and into the sea, forming a valuable estuary and bird sanctuary just south of Monterey Bay, right. Given the rapid rate of disappearing estuaries around the world, a place like Carmel River State Beach gains value every year. WINSTON SWIFT BOYER

A black-tailed jackrabbit, common to grassland areas throughout the state, freezes at the approach of a human before suddenly darting away. D. CAVAGNARO

Founded in 1927, the California State Park System has put many tough years and great accomplishments behind it and now stands before an increasingly prosperous, leisured, and mobile population of 26 million with many tough years ahead. Its dichotomous mandate of having to "provide and protect" is a difficult balancing act. Even within the California Department of Parks and Recreation there are separate divisions for protection and development. That's what Californians want. We want our parks to be authentic yet with some modern conveniences, pristine yet comfortable. We want Aunt Myrtle from Milwaukee to see the old and the wild California, but she needs paved trails (handrails preferred), a clean visitor center, and a nice restaurant. Some parks are wild, some are tame. Some have trails for the blind, wheelchair access for the infirm, sensory discoveries for children, and a variety of other accommodations for visitors of all ages, abilities, races, and languages. They reflect the demands of we the people of California—the ultimate managers of our state parks.

Creating a park is like giving birth; the hardest challenge isn't bringing the child into the world, but raising it properly. The solution is wise management. Yet it's not easy in lean years of budget cuts and understaffing. Dedicated, fifty-hour-a-week rangers struggle just to keep their heads above water.

A "Stewardship 1983" report recognizes "73 types of threats...on the natural and scenic resources...of the California State Park System." Two-thirds of the 300 park units suffer from "intrusive human development, litter, noise, and insufficient staff and money." And over half the units have other ills: "negative visitor behavior, alien plant encroachment, unsafe physical conditions, erosion due to human causes...." The list goes on.

Parks are dynamic places that live in good health and die in poor health. The myth that everything is wonderful in any park system is just that, a myth. California's system is no exception, but it's fighting as hard as it can to keep every one of its units in good health. The support of the people of California is essential.

Since its inception in 1969, the California State Parks Foundation, a private organization, has raised over $60 million for the system. A recent donation was used to buy a "wetlands van" to inform Californians of the importance of rare habitats. One corporate-sponsored program reached over 150,000 school children in one year. "Educating those children," says Randy Jamison, public relations officer for the Department of Parks and Recreation, "is worth any accusation of commercialization. Those are the people who will someday inherit our state park system. It's the greatest heritage we have."

Eighty volunteer associations donate over 300,000 hours a year to the state parks. The guides leading tours through the elephant-seal colonies at Año Nuevo and the men dressed as engineers at the Railroad Museum are volunteers, not rangers. It's an affair of the heart. They have the undying dedication to keep alive a system that above all costs cannot be lessened or lost, for California without her state parks would be a much poorer place. And Californians a much poorer people. This book is the story of California as told through her state parks. It's not a guide, at least not in the strictest sense. The "State Parks Directory" in the back gives the pertinent where's, how's, and when's of the 300 units. *California State Parks* is designed to provoke as much as to inform; to get the reader out there and let the parks speak for themselves. The chapters are organized thematically, not geographically. The first five discuss human history, the second five natural history, and the last two recreation. It's a romping, colorful attempt at the impossible—to sum up in one book California's incredible state park system.

The heritage is ours. It's the best California can give. Discover, learn, enjoy, and respect it. ■

Salt and mist and fog roll into the sea cliffs at San Gregorio State Beach, left, south of Half Moon Bay on the San Francisco peninsula. FRANK S. BALTHIS

Right, sunset paints a cinnabar sky over a beachcomber on a state beach at the north end of Monterey bay, near Santa Cruz. FRANK S. BALTHIS

The early ones

The Indians of California lived in a bountiful land, possessed an excellent knowledge of the resources around them, and moved in small tribes that followed the offerings of the seasons. They had little pottery or agriculture. Territorial imperative, central government, and organized religion were the least of their concerns. They believed in the supernatural and conferred with it through shamans. There was an occasional local feud over the taking of this or a misunderstanding of that, but seldom a tribal war.

Their economies reflected the laws of nature from which they made their daily livings. There was certainly no profit motive or Puritan work ethic. They did enough hunting and gathering to survive comfortably, and no more. The tribes—about 120 of them—were as diverse as California itself. Those on the northern coast were skilled fisherfolk and built economies around salmon, while those in the south relied heavily (but not solely) on an acorn economy.

The Indians of California loved to dance and sing and play their simple musical instruments. Birth, puberty, and marriage were times to celebrate, and death was a time to mourn. Diseases were rare and polygamy was common.

They had lived in California at least 10,000 years, and they numbered between 200,000 and 300,000 when the white man arrived, a population density about five times greater than Indians elsewhere in the United States. Even today more Native Americans live in California than in any other state.

The beginning of the end of the good life came when the Spanish arrived, and the Mexicans and later the Americans finished it off. The newcomers called the Indians "diggers" from the mistaken notion that they lived by grubbing roots only. The Spanish regarded them as a primitive, lethargic, and indolent people compared with the advanced Indian civilizations of Mexico. And Americans, having seen the more aggressive Indians of the Great Plains, agreed with the Spanish.

The bark, conical sweat house at Indian Grinding Rock State Historical Park, left, was called an u'macha' by the Northern Miwoks. GEORGE ELICH

Howard Edwards, a self-taught artist, and his family homesteaded land in the Antelope Valley, right, in 1928. The fields of poppies that start blooming in March and continue to brighten the valley for four to six weeks are just part of the spectacular scenery that Edwards fell in love with. The dream home that he built here now houses the Antelope Valley Indian Museum. CARR CLIFTON

The ocher artwork of Indians, left, is preserved at Lake Perris State Recreation Area, site of the first of several forthcoming regional Indian museums in the California State Park System. CALIFORNIA DEPARTMENT OF PARKS AND RECREATION

Silhouetted against the sky, a cow parsnip, below, has gone to seed and left its umbrella-like skeleton behind. Many California Indians used the seeds, stems, and other parts of this useful plant in their everyday lives. GEORGE WARD

It was easier on the conscience of these newcomers to steal from a people they regarded as lowly.

Dispossessed of their cultures, lands, and languages and subjugated by the self-serving rationales and superior weapons of their conquerors, California's Indians suddenly found themselves kneeling to a foreign god and trespassing on lands they had once walked freely. Measles, smallpox, cholera, and venereal disease—white man's diseases—killed them by the thousands. The padres promised that life in the hereafter would be better, but life in the here-and-now had gotten much worse. Some rebelled and were killed. Others ran away only to find they had no place to go.

Victims of gold paving and soul saving, California's Indians eventually slipped into cultural stews with whites, blacks, Asians, Hispanics, and others, or they retreated into pureblood pockets of native language groups, preserving as best they could the cultures that had sustained them for hundreds of generations.

Some of California's best preserved Native American archaeological sites and *in situ* historical artifacts are in the state parks. Fewer than half a dozen parks focus entirely on the Indians, but over 100 refer to them in one way or another. There are Indian museums, nature trails, artifacts, legends, outdoor crafts, and various other interpretations that add tremendous depth and color to the parks.

The State Indian Museum in Sacramento (next to Sutter's Fort) has many excellent displays on the daily lives and customs of tribes and tribelets from around California. Art, family structure, and spiritual expression are explained. Traditional dress from several dances—the brush, jump, flower, and white deerskin—are on display. Of special interest to most visitors are the clamshells used for money and adornment.

The Antelope Valley Indian Museum (15 miles east of Lancaster) is a structure built more into the land than on top of it, tucked like a nest into the weathered flank of Piute Butte in the Mojave Desert.

Boulders and natural passageways add to the building and, together with a rich collection of artifacts, impart a genuine feeling of Native Americana. There are seven separate roof elevations and two gabled turrets. Once the home of a self-taught artist and architect, it was purchased several decades ago by Grace Oliver, who is largely responsible for the fine collections of weaving, basketry, and the like. When finances looked grim for Ms. Oliver, the State of California came to the rescue, purchased the building, and designated it a museum.

The first of several forthcoming statewide regional Indian museums has been completed at Lake Perris State Recreation Area. Handsome displays portray the lives of Indians in the Mojave Desert from times before the white man arrived, through the years of turmoil, and into their renewed heritage of today. The themes interweave like the strands of a time-honored wool blanket.

Chumash Painted Cave and Indian Grinding Rock are two of the most significant Native American archaeological sites in the California State Park System. The Chumash were a proud, productive, seaworthy people who fished the Santa Barbara Channel and hunted the coastal mountains with great skill. They tell their story with simple, haunting art on the walls of a sandstone cave north of Santa Barbara.

A broad limestone outcropping punctuated by 1,185 mortar cups and 363 petroglyphs (rock carvings) is the centerpiece of Indian Grinding Rock State Historic Park (11 miles from Jackson, southeast of Sacramento). This is where the Northern Miwoks pounded acorns into soups, mush, and patties. (The patties were then baked on hot rocks and eaten like a tortilla or slice of bread.) The park also has a round house, a religious dwelling, and a playing field that further

unveils the lives of the peaceable Miwoks.

The Indians of California were and still are great teachers and learners. Their 135 separate idioms survive in place names and stories preserved in state parks from the redwoods to the Mojave and from the Spanish missions to the gold country. In being the first to arrive, their lifestyles, values, and attitudes have become an index from which those of every other Californian—the latecomers—can be measured.

Going back to the Indians, then, is like going home. The impressions they make should be as deep and as lasting as an acorn-milled cavity in a bed of limestone. ∎

These Miwok Indian mortar cups are evidence worn in stone. The limestone outcropping at Indian Grinding Rock State Historic Park is covered with 1,185 chaw'ses, or mortar cups. The Miwok Indians used the chaw'ses in grinding acorns and other seeds into palatable food.
CARR CLIFTON

The Californios

They came for God, glory, and gold, but not always in that order. They were Spaniards and they came to protect Spanish interests, but in this distant corner of the New World they decided on a new name for themselves: Californios.

Around 1510 the Spanish novelist Garci Rodríguez Ordóñez de Montalvo wrote a book wherein he made several references to a fabled island. "Know ye, that on the right hand of the Indies there is an island called California, very near the Terrestrial Paradise." It was inhabited by black women who carried weapons of gold "for in all the island there was no other metal." If Hernan Cortez and his captains—the plunderers of the Aztecs of Mexico—hadn't read the book, they'd certainly heard of it. And with one conquest behind them they were hungry for more. Thus was born in the avarice of Mexico's conquerors a place of myth or fact—an island in spirit if not in geography—called California.

But rough northerly seas and an unforgiving desert made travel over water and land equally difficult. Not until 250 years after Cortez landed in Mexico did the Spanish establish their first settlement (San Diego) in California.

Inching up the coast, Franciscan friars founded a string of 21 missions, each within a day's walk of the next. These religious communities were, they said, their "great spiritual conquest of the wilderness." Soldiers built presidios (forts) at San Diego, Santa Barbara, Monterey, and San Francisco. Pueblos (civilian towns) followed. Then came great rancheros and the pastoral lives of dons, doñas, and vaqueros. Horses, cattle, sheep, and endless tracts of unfenced land became the riches of the Californio, not gold.

Spain ruled California from 1769 to 1821, and Mexico ruled from 1822 to 1846. Neither one held the distant province in high regard nor was capable of effectively governing it. Under Spain it was the loneliest outpost of a dying empire. And things worsened under Mexico. The Californios grumbled and talked about establishing their independence, but their numbers were small, only about 6,000 in the 1840s. The farsighted among them knew they'd be unable to defend their land from the growing tide of Americans pouring over the mountains.

Don't discount the young when it comes to performing living history demonstrations in Old Town San Diego State Historic Park, left, in the heart of downtown San Diego. Teachers and parents alike recognize that a child can learn more history here in a day than in a month in a classroom. And it's a lot more fun as well.
FRANK S. BALTHIS

Founded in 1823, Mission San Francisco Solano de Sonoma, right, was the last of the 21 Franciscan missions established on El Camino Real. Now part of Sonoma State Historic Park, the mission houses a museum. JEFF GNASS

The Mexican-American War raised the Stars and Stripes over California in July 1846, but what destroyed the Californios was the gold rush two years later. How ironic that the Californios—descendants of the conquistadors who had fleeced the gold and crushed the cultures of the mighty Aztecs and Incas—would miss the placer deposits of the Sierra Nevada. It was the Americans who found the gold this time, and in a powerful twist of fate it was the Spanish Californios whose culture was eventually crushed.

The best preserved and restored pockets of California's Spanish-Mexican Era are in the state park system. The doors of missions, pueblos, and presidios have swung open wide for the public. Taken individually, each is fascinating and fun. But taken altogether they are a rich treasure of a time, a people, and a culture that helped to make California the colorful place it is today.

Old Town San Diego State Historic Park

No finer harbor had met the eyes of the navigator Juan Rodríguez Cabrillo than the one he sailed into on September 28, 1542. He called it San Miguel, but merchant-adventurer Sebastian Vizcaíno found the same lovely spot 60 years later and renamed it San Diego.

One hundred sixty-seven years after that, spurred by reports of Russian activity in the Pacific Basin, Mexico mounted the "Sacred Expedition." Five parties—three by sea and two by land—set

Celebrating the Fourth of July at Old Town San Diego State Historic Park, these volunteers are wearing uniforms from the Mexican War, the Civil War, and the Indian Wars. BILL EVARTS

A blacksmith, left, tends his forge, making the tools necessary for everyday life one hundred years ago in Old Town San Diego. BILL EVARTS

forth in the spring of 1769 for San Diego. One ship disappeared with all hands on board. Another arrived after a relatively smooth voyage of only 54 days. The third ship, leaky, poorly provisioned, and poorly navigated, sailed into San Diego Harbor after 110 days at sea. The scurvy-stricken crew was too weak to lower its boats to go ashore.

When the first land party arrived soon thereafter, they found not a small presidio and camp, but a filthy makeshift sail-tent hospital filled with death and disease. The expedition doctor, himself very sick, would later go insane. It was the second land party, however, that contained the two men necessary to keep the expedition alive: Captain Gaspar de Portolá, the expedition leader, and Father Junípero Serra, father-president of the missions-to-be in California.

In *California, An Interpretive History*, author Walton Bean says Father Serra "was a vigorous, hard-driving man, never turning back from a task he had begun, always demanding the full measure of work from others as well as from himself. In physical stature, Serra was short, not more than 5 feet 2 or 3 inches in height—but in courage and determination, he was a giant." He was 55 years old when he arrived at San Diego in 1769, and until his death in 1784 he would establish the first nine of California's 21 Franciscan missions.

Spain had chosen the Franciscans over the Jesuits to Christianize California thinking the former would be less inclined to meddle in politics. They were wrong. Father Serra and his padres had work to do, and if accomplishing it meant knocking heads with local Spanish officials, then so be it. The first mission in California—San Diego de Alcalá—was founded on July 16, 1769.

The local Tapai Indians grumbled at the Spanish invasion. Padres insisted they move to the mission where they'd live and learn Christianity and agriculture, which they did. But they were punished for infractions they didn't understand, they caught lethal European diseases, and their women fell prey to drunken Spanish soldiers. Frustrated

Two venerated homes, La Casa de Estudillo (right) and La Casa de Bandini (left), stand side by side in Old Town San Diego. Spanish society evolved around them in the days when José Antonio Estudillo and Juan Bandini regaled friends and family with tales of romance and adventure.
BILL EVARTS

and angry, the Indians revolted in 1775, attacked and burned the mission, and killed a padre.

Slowly, though, San Diego matured into a livable place. The Indians surrendered their lives and freedoms to a civilization that would never fully integrate them, and by 1800 an estimated 1,500 lived at Mission San Diego.

Most of the Spaniards (about 160) lived in the presidio six miles west on a hill near the coast. As soldiers retired and began to till lands outside presidial boundaries, a pueblo emerged. A plaza was laid out in the early 1820s, and the settlement of Old Town San Diego grew steadily while the presidio, starved of supplies and reinforcements, fell into decline.

Mexico had won her independence from Spain and trade embargos were dropped. European and Yankee ships did a lively business along the coast, trading whatever they had for prized cowhides,

called "California banknotes."

One who prospered was José Antonio Estudillo. A son of a former captain of the presidio, Estudillo lived a life of frontier luxury with his wife, seven sons, and five daughters in an incongruous world of cool chambers, velvet draperies, mahogany bedsteads, rich tapestries, and silver candelabras. When Commodore Robert F. Stockton raised the American flag over San Diego in 1846, the Estudillos and other San Diegans merely went on about their lives.

The bigger changes came in 1857 when the Butterfield Overland Mail route bypassed San Diego for Los Angeles, and again in 1872 when a fire gutted the old pueblo and coincided with a campaign to start a new downtown along the waterfront.

Decades of care and renovation have preserved Old Town San Diego. In fact, it has more life now than it ever had. Four million people a year pass through this state historic park. Spanish facades conceal modern shops, boutiques, and restaurants. Mariachi bands play in the streets while visitors sip margaritas the size of grapefruits. There is a visitor center, a playhouse, and a plaza, plus many casas from the bygone days, including the famous Casa de Estudillo. Also worth seeing is the San Diego Union Building, which was prefabricated in Maine and shipped around South America in 1851. Probably the most popular spot, though, is the "Bazaar del Mundo"—Market Place of the World—that sells everything from French finery to Irish crystal to Mexican pottery.

Father Serra, forgive us, for Old Town San Diego is a far cry from what you might have envisioned. But you're not forgotten, nor are your dreams. Beneath the fleeting fashions and freeway traffic is the colorful past of a sacred and timeless San Diego.

Monterey State Historic Park

Monterey needs no introduction. Perched on the shore like a latter-day siren, it condenses the salty essence of California's coastal history into a comfortable blend of crooked streets, waterfronts, and white adobe buildings. Robert Louis Stevenson called it "the Old Pacific Capital." And John Steinbeck, in his 1945 classic *Cannery Row* called the Monterey waterfront "a poem, a stink, a grating noise, a quality of light, a tone, a habit, a nostalgia, a dream." Aside from the stink and the noise, it's still all there.

In December 1602, eighteen years before the Pilgrims landed at Plymouth Rock, Sebastian Vizcaino sailed into a broad bay and named it for the Spanish viceroy of Mexico, Conde de Monterey. Interested more in his promotion than his accuracy, Vizcaino described the bay as a fine harbor "sheltered from all winds" and flanked with an abundance of timber. When Captain Gaspar de Portolá stood on the exposed shore of Monterey Bay 167 years later, he could hardly believe it was the same place. Nevertheless, in 1770 he built a presidio while the indomitable Father Junípero Serra founded San Carlos Borromeo de Carmelo, California's second mission.

Monterey was on the map. For the next eight decades Spain and Mexico made Monterey their provincial capital.

Monterey State Historic Park consists of several well-preserved nineteenth-century adobe structures "whose protruding beams, covered balconies, and red tile roofs," writes James Armstrong in National Geographic *Traveler* Magazine, "lend a beguiling, fly-in-amber quality to the place." The Customhouse (next to Fisherman's Wharf) is a distillation of times and events pivotal in California history. Revenues from shipping poured through here into the provincial Mexican coffers until on July 7, 1846, Commodore John Drake Sloat raised the Stars and Stripes for the first time over California. The past is never far away in Monterey; just take a walk down a street and use a little imagination.

The barking of sea lions, the memorable passages of novelist John Steinbeck, and the photographs of stilted, rustic canneries and homes all symbolize Monterey's Fisherman's Wharf. In the 1830s and 1840s, when San Francisco was nothing more than a quiet presidio and a few shanties, Monterey was a proud, bustling capital where Yankee clipper ships dropped anchor regularly to do a lively trade with Mexican merchants and dons. The wharf today is home port to a commercial fishing fleet and attracts tourists from across the country. ED COOPER

El Pueblo de Los Angeles State Historic Park

Felipe de Nêvé was disturbed. As Spanish governor of California he was responsible for the success, or failure, of the missions, presidios, and general Hispanic settlement in his province. But things weren't going well. By late 1777, after eight missions had been founded, the Franciscan friars began to protest giving their food to the presidio soldiers. The soldiers, in turn, had begun to harass the missions.

Nêvé's solution was to establish two self-supporting pueblos, one in the north and one in the south. Thus, on a large plain of the Porciuncula River, near the Indian village of Yang-Na, Nêvé personally chose the site of what would become El Pueblo de Nuestra Señora la Reina de los Angeles del Rio de Porciuncula, or The Town of Our Lady the Queen of the Angels by the River of Porciuncula. Four years later, in 1781, while George Washington was accepting the British surrender that ended the American Revolutionary War, 44 people of Spanish, African, and Indian blood settled into their new pueblo, Los Angeles. It was the second town founded in California (behind San Jose).

The original site was abandoned in 1815 when a flood forced the town to move to higher ground where El Pueblo de Los Angeles State Historic Park stands today. Officials feel that no student in the Los Angeles public schools has had a complete education until he or she has walked through the brick and adobe world of Olvera Street in the heart of the pueblo. Next to the Tunini Winery and across from Sepulveda House, both

Mission San Juan Bautista was founded in 1797 on what was later to become an important stop on the Los Angeles-San Francisco stagecoach route. Despite damage from earthquakes, the mission church has been in continuous use since its completion in 1812. The mission along with its satellite buildings are now preserved as San Juan Bautista State Historic Park.
JEFF GNASS

Captain George Vancouver wasn't impressed with the Spanish in California. He regarded them as disorganized and incapable of cleanliness, but his impressions softened in Santa Barbara in 1793 when he wrote, "The presidio excels all others in neatness and...essential comforts." The last presidio founded by the Spanish in California (after San Diego, Monterey, and San Francisco), El Presidio de Santa Barbara was a quadrangle of exciting and enterprising civilization on a wilderness coast.

A simple chapel stood opposite the main gate, and the Spanish flag flew in the middle of the parade grounds. Fortified with two cannon bastions and two defense walls and lined with stables, shops, and family quarters, the presidio was the district military headquarters for the area between San Luis Obispo and El Pueblo de Los Angeles. Father Junípero Serra blessed the site and its founding in April 1782.

Five buildings still stand along East Cañon Perdido Street in the middle of downtown Santa Barbara. El Cuartel, built in 1782 as a house for soldiers and their families, is the oldest building in the state park system and the second oldest in all California. Its living room has been converted into an attractive museum. Flanking the reconstructed chapel are the Cañedo Adobe and the quarters where visiting padres stayed.

All together, only about one-eighth of the presidio remains, and despite its well-preserved earthy milieu, the contrast between then and now is striking.

But Santa Barbarans love their city and respect their past. It's the only one of four Spanish presidios still standing, and they're not about to let it fall.

La Purísima Mission State Historic Park

Nowhere in California does the Spanish Era come more alive than at La Purísima Mission.

built in the 1880s, is the Avila Adobe. Built in 1818, it's the oldest building in Los Angeles. Commodore Stockton made his headquarters here when he captured Los Angeles from the Californios in January 1847. Avila Adobe later became a boarding house and was even a restaurant for awhile.

By 1860 over 4,000 people lived in El Pueblo de Los Angeles. Bull fights ended and baseball games were organized. Brick replaced adobe. The Americanization of Los Angeles had begun. But it was still a sleepy town as most of California's growth in the late 1800s (spurred by gold and railroads) occurred in the north around Sacramento and especially San Francisco.

Restoration initiated recently for the 1981 bicentennial has imparted new life into El Pueblo de Los Angeles. For residents and visitors in this massive, sprawling city, it's refreshing to find an attractive, compact, and culturally rich pueblo where one can sit in the plaza beneath a huge Moreton Bay fig (planted in the 1870s) and contemplate the footsteps of those who passed this way long before.

El Presidio de Santa Barbara State Historic Park

A bell hangs from a wooden beam at La Purísima Mission, top, the most completely restored of California's 21 Spanish missions. FRANK S. BALTHIS

Inside La Purísima Mission, bottom, the outside light and heat surrender to a dim coolness. As many as a thousand Chumash Indians would crowd in here for Catholic services. FRANK S. BALTHIS

Tucked into a canyon above the Santa Inez River outside the city of Lompoc, La Purísima wears its history proudly. It's the most completely restored of California's 21 missions.

Images come to mind easily while strolling along the three-quarter-mile-long trail from building to building, beneath adobe archways, over brick and tile walkways, past a fountain, and through a garden of figs, grapes, peppers, olives, and pears. Life had its ups and downs here; its periods of prosperity and austerity. There were times of great joy and times of great sadness. From its founding in 1787 to its secularization in 1834, La Purísima weathered numerous earthquakes, fires, droughts, diseases, and financial woes, as well as a month-long uprising of the Chumash Indians.

Once a proud, prosperous, and friendly people, the Chumash absorbed one indignity after another until they could take no more. Their revolt ended when soldiers from the presidio in Monterey marched down El Camino Real to La Purísima, killed 16 Chumash, and restored an uneasy peace. Could the Indians be blamed? In one three-year period over 500 had died of smallpox and measles. Fear and disillusionment had become a way of life. The men worked in the fields sunup to sundown for meager meals

With all due respect to the Franciscans, the blunt day-to-day truth was that they spearheaded the imposition of one culture onto another. Yet in a land and time when the arrival of westward moving Europeans was inevitable, it's probably best that the first vanguard to hit California and the Chumash were the good-hearted, well-meaning, and hard-working Franciscans. They, too, worked sunup to sundown in the fields and ate meager meals. They truly loved the Chumash people, and the Chumash eventually came to appreciate the Franciscans. Perhaps it was learning to accept an obvious fate. The Spaniards were here to stay.

Music was a favorite occupation for everyone at La Purísima. The Indians would sing into the night and ring the church bells with great enthusiasm. They planted numerous crops, installed sophisticated irrigation systems, and made soap, candles, wool, and leather goods.

The events that unfolded in far away Spain and Mexico—mismanagement, apathy, and revolution—sent political and economic shock waves through California that were completely out of the hands of the friars.

After secularization, La Purísima was abandoned and fell into decay. One hundred years later it was rescued and restored by the Civilian Conservation Corps beginning in 1934.

San Juan Baustista State Historic Park

San Juan Baustista, north of Salinas, greets visitors with a proud and weathered warmth. History lingers here. A gardener works beneath the balconies of the Castro House and the Plaza Hall. A robed priest shuffles down a rock and tile walkway. Across the plaza is the Monastery Wing and the 175-year-old mission church, a veteran of many earthquakes, still owned and operated by the Catholic church. The mossy red tiles and cracked archways wear their years graciously. Huddled around the old plaza, the buildings still convey the strong sense of protection and security that has made the little town and mission a refuge since its founding in 1797.

Among the legendary residents and visitors here were Angelo Zanetta, who built the Plaza Hotel and was reputed to be the finest host in California; John C. Frémont, who provisioned his 400-man California Battalion before marching south; and the notorious Tiburcio Vasquez, foremost among Californio banditos, who stole the hearts of Mexican women and the horses of American men. Such is the charm of San Juan Bautista.

San Pasqual Battlefield State Historic Park

The morning of December 6, 1846, dawned cold

The colors of spring brighten the plaza around San Juan Bautista, where the Catholic Church still owns and operates the mission church and conducts services. GEORGE WUERTHNER

and foggy near the Indian village of San Pasqual, 35 miles northeast of San Diego. Stephen Watts Kearny, commanding general of the United States Army of the West, was awakened by Kit Carson, who informed him that a detachment of rebel Californios under General Andres Pico was nearby. Carson urged immediate battle, assuring Kearny that the Californios were nothing more than spineless farmers unwilling and unable to fight. Kearny swallowed the advice. (If he couldn't trust Kit Carson, who could he trust?) He roused his tired, travel-weary men and charged through the fog. Little did Kearny realize that he was about to launch a critical battle in the California theater of the Mexican-American War.

The war had erupted in April 1846 when the expansionist plans of President James K. Polk collided with Mexico's rejection of the U.S. annexation of Texas. Many Californios had refused to get involved, but the uncivil ways of Americans like Captain John C. Frémont infuriated them, and they took up arms out of anger and insult.

During the summer months of 1846, landing parties from the U.S. Navy had captured San Francisco, Monterey, Santa Barbara, Los Angeles, and San Diego. Commodore Stockton had sent Carson east to inform Washington officials that California was "peacefully and firmly in American hands." Carson met Kearny enroute, and upon hearing the news Kearny dispatched all but 100 of his men to join General Zachary Taylor on the battlefields of Mexico. Meanwhile, however, the Californios had retaken Los Angeles and had threatened the Americans in San Diego.

Southern California was filled with insurrection when Kearny's army finally arrived after crossing the Colorado Desert. With practically all their cavalry mounts dead, they rode on mules or unbroken horses. And here they were in San Pasqual on a chilly December morning, charging across unknown terrain on untrained mounts after a misjudged adversary.

General Pico and his Californios took flight until the Americans were spread out widely on their mounts. The Californios then turned, attacked and overpowered and outmaneuvered the Americans.

The fighting didn't last long. When Pico withdrew, leaving Kearny and his men on the field, 22 Americans were dead or dying and only one Californio. Kearny himself was twice wounded. He described the Californios as "admirably mounted and the very best riders in the world; hardly one that is not fit for the circus." Yet because Kearny held his ground and remained on the battlefield, he claimed San Pasqual as an American victory. (A few more such "victories" and the American forces in California would have been in trouble.)

Pico and his brave Californios clearly won the battle of San Pasqual, but it would be Mexican California's swan song.

The Americans recaptured Los Angeles on January 10, 1847, and three days later Pico surrendered to Frémont at Cahuenga. In an uncharacteristic act, Frémont extended a complete pardon to all the Californio rebels. A new era had begun. After 77 years under Spanish and Mexican rule, California belonged to the United States. But the proud Californios never forgot the Battle of San Pasqual.

Pio Pico State Historic Park

Hanging on a wall in Pio Pico State Historic Park in Whittier is a painting that depicts a sullen, stormy sky over a small, weathered rancho. The muddy street is pooled with water from a recent rain. The trees are dark and leafless. A black horse, its head bowed low, stands hitched to a black buggy in front of the porch. Two women stand at the doorway, one covered with a shawl, her head down, the other holding a handkerchief to her eyes. Walking toward the buggy, slumped at the shoulders and gripping a cane, is an old man with a white beard. Like the sky, the trees, and the buggy that will carry him away, he's dressed in black. His posture shows defeat, his expression sadness. He is 90-year-old Pio Pico, once one of California's greatest landowners and political and economic figures, always an overly generous man, now penniless and alone and being evicted from his home, El Ranchito, by a certain but unprovable case of legal fraud. The painting portrays not just the end of a person, but the end of a people. Artist Herbert Hahn calls it *The Sad Day.*

The path of the padres

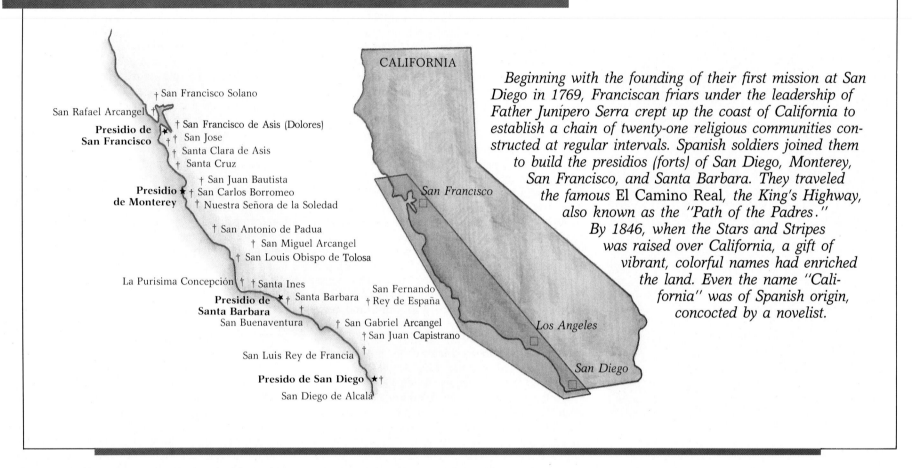

CALIFORNIA

† San Francisco Solano

San Rafael Arcangel †

Presidio de San Francisco ★† San Francisco de Asis (Dolores)
†† San Jose
† Santa Clara de Asis
† Santa Cruz

† San Juan Bautista
Presidio de Monterey ★† San Carlos Borromeo
† Nuestra Señora de la Soledad

† San Antonio de Padua
† San Miguel Arcangel
† San Louis Obispo de Tolosa

La Purisima Concepción † † Santa Ines
Presidio de Santa Barbara ★† Santa Barbara
San Buenaventura † San Gabriel Arcangel
† San Juan Capistrano

San Fernando † Rey de España

San Luis Rey de Francia †

Presido de San Diego ★†
San Diego de Alcala

San Francisco

Los Angeles

San Diego

Beginning with the founding of their first mission at San Diego in 1769, Franciscan friars under the leadership of Father Junípero Serra crept up the coast of California to establish a chain of twenty-one religious communities constructed at regular intervals. Spanish soldiers joined them to build the presidios (forts) of San Diego, Monterey, San Francisco, and Santa Barbara. They traveled the famous El Camino Real, *the King's Highway, also known as the "Path of the Padres."*
By 1846, when the Stars and Stripes was raised over California, a gift of vibrant, colorful names had enriched the land. Even the name "California" was of Spanish origin, concocted by a novelist.

Pio Pico State Historic Park, near the intersection of Whittier Boulevard and the San Gabriel River Freeway (605), a little southeast of central Los Angeles, preserves the home and commemorates the life of a man who helped shape six decades of California history.

Pio Pico's life began as it ended, in poverty. The son of a soldier, he was determined to make a better life for himself and his seven brothers and sisters. He excelled in early business ventures, won election to the *diputación* (the legislative ad-

visory board to the governor), and in 1845 he became Mexican California's last governor. Together with his brother Andres, he gained title to over half a million acres of land, including half of the San Fernando Valley and several large ranchos, making him one of the richest men in California.

But Pico's frivolous habits and lack of good judgment undermined his wealth. He sold his San Fernando Valley land in 1868 for $180,000, used half the earnings to build the elegant Pico House Hotel

(in El Pueblo de Los Angeles) and finally sold the hotel for only $15,000.

The historian Howard Holter writes, "He spent money lavishly, bought whatever caught his fancy, was overgenerous, and had a passion for horse racing and gambling. Piece by piece, he sold off his vast holdings to pay debts and raise more money. In 1883, a lawyer named Bernard Cohn struck the final ignominious blow. Pico signed what he believed was a loan, backed by his rancho and other holdings. Cohn claimed, however, that Pico had given him a deed of sale. The dispute resulted in a widely publicized court case, *Pico v. Cohn*, in which the court decided against Pico, even though it was the general opinion of lawyers at the time that he was the victim of an outrageous fraud." Pico went to live with his adopted daughter, Joaquina Moreno, on West 15th Street in Los Angeles. He died two years later in September 1894.

Pio Pico is gone, but continuing renovation of El Ranchito promises all visitors that a light into the life of this early figure in Los Angeles and California will shine a long, long time.

Sonoma and Petaluma Adobe State Historic Parks

Mariano Guadalupe Vallejo, soldier, statesman, and scholar, carried history on his back when he rode into California's northern frontier in 1833. He was no ordinary 25-year-old Mexican military man. He was a smooth-tempered thinker surrounded by hot-headed expansionists and cold-blooded bureaucrats. He foresaw the inevitable and forgave the impetuous, and when he died at age 82 in Sonoma in 1890, he had the respect of citizens throughout the state. California sparkles here and there from his influence, but nowhere more so than in Petaluma Adobe and Sonoma, the places he called home.

Vallejo traveled north to investigate the Russians at Fort Ross and Bodega Bay. Two years later he returned to secularize Mission San Francisco Solano at Sonoma, the last and northernmost of California's 21 missions, on orders from the governor. He than started colonies at Petaluma and

Santa Rosa, and on land formerly owned by the mission, he founded the town called Sonoma. For a reward he was given ten leagues of land (44,000 acres) in the Petaluma Valley to develop his private rancho. In a short time Vallejo's holdings grew to make him one of California's largest landowners. He owned most of the fertile land in the Sonoma Valley where his 50,000 head of cattle, 24,000 sheep, and 8,000 horses lived on several ranchos totaling a quarter-million acres.

In 1835 he built a big adobe house, La Casa Grande, on the plaza at Sonoma and moved his wife and young son there from San Francisco. La Casa Grande, as much a fortress as a home with its watchtower, walls, and private 40-man standing army, became the nucleus of social and diplomatic life north of San Francisco. Eleven Vallejo children were born there.

Over the next ten years an increasing number of Americans arrived in California. The first wagon train crossed the Sierra Nevada in 1841, and more came each year thereafter. Several leading

Built from 1836 to 1846 on a knoll overlooking 100 square miles of an agricultural empire, Petaluma Adobe typified the ambitions and abilities of General Mariano Vallejo, a man incapable of doing anything in a small way, especially ranching. MARIANNE AUSTIN-McDERMON

Lachryma Montis, the retirement home of General Mariano Vallejo, rests in ageless splendor outside Sonoma. Vallejo, one of California's most famous Mexican citizens of the late 1800s, lived his final years here, writing his ten-volume History of California, *reading some of his 12,000 books, playing the piano, and tending his vineyards. The house was built from 1851 to 1852 and serves today as a museum and interpretive center for the Vallejo Home unit of Sonoma State Historic Park.* ED COOPER

Californios suggested that Mexico form an alliance with England or France to stem the disturbing tide of rowdy foreigners. But it was Vallejo alone who realized the power of the American Manifest Destiny—that the United States would someday claim California and bridge the Atlantic and Pacific shores.

How ironic it was, then, when 33 angry American settlers descended upon the village of Sonoma on June 14, 1846, surrounded Vallejo's unguarded home, and announced that he was a prisoner of war. "What war?" Vallejo responded. The retired Mexican general passed around bottles of *aguardiente* while the filibusters fumbled for an answer. They eventually accused Vallejo of land inequities and hauled him off to Sutter's Fort where John C. Frémont threw him in a cell for two months.

Meanwhile, the insurgents in Sonoma raised a makeshift flag of white cloth emblazoned with a red star and a grizzly bear above a red-flannel band with the black letters CALIFORNIA REPUBLIC. This was the famous Bear Flag Revolt. The design of the original banner was adopted by the California Legislature in 1911 as the state flag.

By the time Vallejo was released in August 1846, the Mexican-American War was raging. Monterey had fallen to the U.S. Navy, and the Stars and Stripes was waving over his old headquarters in Sonoma. Large tracts of his land had been sequestered, including thousands of his livestock. His great riches seriously reduced, Vallejo reportedly burned his Mexican uniforms, shaved his heavy beard, and gracefully accepted his fate.

Petaluma Adobe was the heart of the original land grant given to Vallejo. Later enlarged from 10 leagues to 15 leagues (66,000 acres), the rancho spread from San Pablo Bay north to Glen Ellen between Petaluma and Sonoma creeks.

After the Mexican-American War, Vallejo lost nearly everything to American squatters who pilfered the adobe and rancho of his prized possessions.

The adobe was purchased in 1910 and preserved until 1951 by the Petaluma Chapter of the Native Sons of the Golden West. The state then took title of the building, replaced the roof after a windstorm, and has since restored many of the rooms with furniture and exhibits from the rancho period. Mariano Vallejo would be proud; his youth, strength, and riches live today within the walls of Petaluma Adobe.

Although he was a delegate to California's

constitutional convention in 1848, was elected to the state senate in 1850, and was elected mayor of Sonoma in 1852 and again in 1860, Vallejo never prospered in the American period as he had in the Mexican. He spent his last 35 years with his beloved wife at his retirement estate, Lachryma Montis, just west of Sonoma and preserved today as the Vallejo Home unit of Sonoma State Historic Park.

Life wasn't what it used to be, but it wasn't bad either. Despite having lost all but 280 acres of his original half million, Vallejo himself was happy. Bitterness was beneath him. "I had my day," he said, "It was a proud one."

In 1883 the aging poet Walt Whitman, veritable champion of American democracy and the common man, reflected on the Spanish and Mexican influence in California.

"To that composite American identity of the future," he wrote, "Spanish character will supply some of the most needed parts. No stock shows a grander historical perspective—grander in religiousness and loyalty, or for patriotism, courage, decorum, gravity, and honor. . . . Who knows but that element, like the course of some subterranean river, dipping invisibly for a hundred or two years, is now to emerge in broadest flow and permanent action?"

Indeed, that river is emerging. The people of California, especially the growing number of Hispanics, find it in themselves whenever they visit the missions, presidios, and pueblos preserved for all generations in state historic parks. ▪

Every spring the California state flower, California poppy (Eschscholzia californica), paints the landscapes of several state parks with brilliant yellows and oranges.
D. CAVAGNARO

Gold fever

"GOLD," read the headlines of the San Francisco *Californian* in 1848. "The whole country . . . resounds with the sordid cry of gold, Gold, GOLD while the field is left half planted, the house half built, and everything is neglected but the manufacture of shovels and pickaxes."

The California gold rush was one of the zaniest, wildest, and most colorful chapters in American history. A generation of brash young men—most of them citizens of a brash young nation—headed for the foothills of the Sierra Nevada to find their El Dorado. Most worked hard for little reward but ultimately discovered that the richest element was not the gold, but the search itself.

A half-dozen state parks chronicle the gold rush in all its character and charm, from the placers at Coloma to the tunnels at the Empire to the hydraulics at Malakoff. These are stories of the people who by good luck and bad luck, sweet dreams and broken dreams, found a grand adventure and a new home and laid a golden cornerstone in the history of the state of California.

Marshall Gold Discovery State Historic Park

On January 24, 1848, James Marshall, a carpenter and millwright, was on his morning inspection of John Sutter's partially completed sawmill on the South Fork of the American River, when he made a discovery that would catapult California out of obscurity and into the headlines of newspapers around the world.

"It was a clear cold morning," Marshall would recall years later. "I shall never forget that morning as I was taking my usual walk along the race after shutting off the water, my eye was caught with a glimpse of something shiny in the bottom of the ditch. There was about a foot of water running then. I reached down and picked it up. It made my heart thump, for I was certain it was gold."

No bigger than a small pebble, the nugget in Marshall's hand was worth probably less than 50 cents. But he found others. Placing them in the crown of his hat, Marshall walked back to the mill where a dozen or so men were working. "Boys," he said, hardly believing his own words, "I believe I've found a gold mine." Four days later Marshall galloped into Sutter's Fort and burst in upon his surprised employer.

Adjacent to Marshall Gold Discovery State Historic Park, two amateur gold seekers, left, stand ankle deep in the American River pouring sand, gravel, and water through a sluice box, and hoping against the odds that the argonauts of 150 years ago might have missed some grains of gold.
WILLIAM HELSEL

Built in 1878, the Mohawk Stamp Mill, right, stands among manzanita, ceanothus and buckthorn above the ghost town of Johnsville at Plumas-Eureka State Park. More then 400 men worked here and at other mills during the 1870s and 1880s, prying gold out of the tunnels in Eureka Peak. Year by year the mining operations tapered off until they were entirely discontinued in 1943. LARRY ULRICH

Don't give up hope. This amateur miner shows his best nugget, taken from the American River in the Coloma Valley, not far from where James Marshall discovered gold in 1848. WILLIAM HELSEL

"He took out a rag from his pocket," Sutter later wrote. "Opening it carefully, he held it before me in his hand. It contained what might have been an ounce and a half of gold dust, flakes, and grains. The biggest piece was not as large as a pea, and it varied from that down to less than a pinhead in size."

Sutter and his assistant, John Bidwell, ran tests with nitric acid, lye, and measuring scales. They hammered the yellow metal, trying to break it. But it would only bend or flatten out. Sure enough, this was pure gold. Little then could either Marshall or Sutter imagine the demise that lay before him. Marshall would end up a penniless alcoholic selling his autograph on dirty frontier streets for whiskey money. Captain John Sutter would tumble into bankruptcy after his employees abandoned his land, his livestock, and his sawmill for the gold.

The news spread slowly at first. California was a sleepy place and it would take a little time to wake up. Rumors began to spread but nobody really believed them. Folks had heard talk of gold before, and that's all it had been, just talk. Meanwhile, a few lucky men at Sutter's Mill quietly filled their pockets.

It took just one shrewd man with a big mouth and a dash of panache to start the fever. Enter Sam Brannan. After filling his store near the discovery site with everything a miner could want or need, he then carried a small bottle of nuggets to San Francisco. Riding his horse up and down Montgomery Street, he brandished the bottle and yelled, "Gold! Gold on the American River." The town went crazy. According to one account, "The blacksmith dropped his hammer, the carpenter his plane, the mason his trowel, the farmer his sickle, the baker his loaf, the tapster his bottle.

"All were off for the mines, some on carts, some on crutches, one even went in a litter." The rush was on.

Except for a few men who straggled down from the Oregon Territory or up from Mexico, the rush of 1848 was feasted upon by Californians only.

The outside world had no idea that the rumors were true. California's population had packed up and moved from the coast to the Sierra foothills. Sonoma, Santa Cruz, San Francisco, and Monterey were emptied of their able-bodied men.

The spring and summer of 1848 were grand times for the gold seekers. Practically anyone with a pan in his hand found gold. And many simply stumbled upon it. In their book, *California Gold*, Phyllis and Lou Zauner write, "A man named McKnight chased a runaway cow, stubbed his toe on an outcropping of quartz, and sure enough, there was a fortune. A German struck a three-ounce nugget while digging a hole for a tent pole. Three Frenchmen uprooted a tree stump from the middle of the Coloma road and dug $5,000 in gold from the hole. A prospector staked out his mule for the night; when he pulled the stake in the morning the hole was gleaming with gold." Probably the most famous tale, though, recalls a burial service a group of miners held for a deceased friend. As they bowed their heads in prayer, they noticed gold flakes in the freshly dug grave. The service was postponed and their friend set aside as the miners grabbed their shovels and went to work.

Crime was no problem that year. As one miner said, "Why steal another fella's gold when it's easier to dig it up yourself." A pick or shovel lying on the ground was honored by common law as a claim marker. And a line of clean laundry (more rare than gold in the Coloma Valley) could be left hanging safely in an unguarded camp.

Sam Brannan and a few others mastered the profitable art of mining the miners, selling shovels, picks, and washpans at a 1,500 percent markup. Colonel R. B. Mason, on assignment with the U.S. Army to investigate mining activities in California, would later report that "Brannan & Company had received in payment or goods $36,000 worth of gold from the first of May to the tenth of July 1848." Adjusted to today's standards, Brannan's fortune was worth a million.

America discovered California's secret that winter when Colonel Mason delivered his report back East and President James K. Polk delivered his State of the Union message, saying, "The

The original Sutter's Mill is gone—washed away down the American River—but this life-size replica stands on higher ground today at Marshall Gold Discovery State Historic Park.
WILLIAM HELSEL

accounts of the abundance of gold in that territory are of such an extraordinary character as would scarcely command belief." Well, "command belief" they did. One of the greatest human migrations in history was headed for California.

Wagon trains over a mile long crept across the Great Plains. Ships from around the world disembarked their motley, gold-hungry passengers in the frenzied, rutted streets of San Francisco. By the spring of 1849 makeshift miners were clambering through the Coloma Valley like termites in a termitarium. Where 2,000 had worked Coloma in 1848, 10,000 worked there in 1849. The once crime-free valley became a nest for long-sleeved gamblers with their marked cards, loaded dice, and false weights. Merchants jacked their prices up even higher. Men of different nationalities, languages, and temperaments, but all with the same dream to get rich quick, slept, ate, and panned side by side. Standing ankle deep in the frigid water, they worked from sunup to sundown six days a week.

The gold became more and more difficult to find. Men soon realized that Marshall's discovery site in the Coloma Valley was not the place to be. The whole Sierra Nevada was rich with gold, they said, and they moved on to Hangtown (Placerville), Auburn, Volcano, Grass Valley, Columbia, and Angels Camp.

So quickly did things quiet down on the South Fork of the American River that a visitor in 1851 called Coloma "the dullest mining town in the whole country."

Sutter's Mill lived a short life. High operating costs and constant theft of its timbers by gold seekers forced it to shut down by May 1849.

And who in his right mind would come to the American River to work at a sawmill? This was Gold Country, by God, where only idiots worked for wages. The river flooded several times and by 1853 the old mill was buried and gone.

The original mill site is marked today by a simple rock and mortar wall standing on the banks of the American River. On higher ground a new mill has been built to the exact dimensions (60 feet long, 39 feet high and 20 feet wide) of the original, complete with a waterwheel (powered by electricity, not running water) and a saw. And next to the mill rests the town of Coloma. Shaded by locust and mimosa, it offers visitors a peaceful respite from the busy world that has passed it by.

Columbia State Historic Park

Columbia is the boomtown that never busted. It's come close, but time after time its wild and lusty history has kept it alive. Never a ghost town, it has been designated a state historic park as one of the best-preserved of the gold rush towns.

Oh, there are ghosts here, like the fellow who was shot and killed over a crooked poker deal at the St. Charles Saloon and Big Annie, keeper of the back street fandango parlor, who embarrassed a proper schoolmarm and got her comeuppance when the volunteer fire department literally washed her out of town. But that is only part of the charm, for Columbia is one of those rare places that has managed to balance its past with a vibrant present.

Tourists walk the streets today with as much life as the gold seekers did over a century ago. The red brick, wrought-iron buildings have been restored to impart a feeling of bygone days. The Fallon Hotel and Theater, probably the most attractive building in town, still echoes the voice of Edwin Booth (brother of John Wilkes Booth, assassinator of Abraham Lincoln) when he played Shakespeare's *Richard III*. The most popular performer, though, was Lola Montez, the former mistress of the King of Bavaria (so she said) who rolled into town with a suitcase of low-cut velvet gowns to perform her tabletop spider dance for an audience of mesmerized miners.

Dr. Thaddeus Hildreth and some friends were the lucky men who stuck their shovels into the red earth of Kennebec Hill in March 1850 and pulled out 30 pounds of gold nuggets in an hour. The news spread "faster than lice" and in less than a month the shantytown of Hildreth's Diggings was home to 5,000 optimists. Lack of running water almost killed the miners' momentum, but with ingenuity and money, the water problem was solved and the population boomed to 20,000. Thus was born Columbia.

Like most gold-mining towns, Columbia was a tinderbox. Two fires in three years gutted half the buildings. Red brick slowly replaced the wooden structures, and with the help of a volunteer fire department, a new Columbia evolved. It had 143 gambling palaces, 30 saloons, a dozen fandango (Mexican dancing) parlors, two theaters (one of them Chinese with 30 Oriental actors), four banks, and eight hotels. Big spenders found their mecca here. Fortunes were won and lost routinely in a night. Down at the Wells Fargo Bank, $55 million in gold was measured ounce by ounce over the years on scales so accurate the miners said "they'd show the weight of a pencil mark on paper."

When the rompin' and rollickin' finally ended, $87 million in gold had been clawed from the earth

around Columbia. It was time to leave. The miners, most of them living in sandwiched shanties that lined the road from Columbia to Sonora, simply packed up and left. But they had given Columbia enough historical color to last hundreds of years.

A progressive California passed Columbia by, building roadways, highways, and railways elsewhere. The town slept in a quiet fold of the Sierra foothills until 1945 when the State of California created Columbia State Historic Park.

Visitors today can still order a sarsaparilla from a bartender who fancies himself a part-time gunslinger. The cotton candy is still made from the same gold rush formulas. One can ride a stagecoach, pan for gold, read the *Columbia Gazette* (founded in 1855), and attend the summertime theater where college students rival the likes of Edwin Booth and Lola Montez.

It's a restful place now, brightened with butterflies and wildflowers in summer and covered by a peaceful snowy blanket in winter. But the flavor of gold and all the characters who chased it will linger as long as the buildings stand.

Empire Mine State Historic Park

The time had come to go underground. "Free gold," the stuff found in streams, rivers, and in surface sediments and removed by panning, sluicing, or digging was gone. In the years ahead the miners would don hardhats, tunnel into the earth, and enter the nether regions of hard-rock gold mining. And if they were lucky, they might get a job at one of California's deepest, richest, and most famous gold-quartz mines: the Empire.

Like most gold discoveries, the Empire was found by accident. George Roberts, a lumberman, stumbled upon the flecks of yellow metal while surveying trees where the Empire Mine parking lot is today. It was the autumn of 1850. Roberts hardly knew what to do as his discovery went public and gold seekers flooded in to stake their claims. They quickly realized, however, that placer (surface) claims were of no value here. This gold wasn't in a valley bottom where it had been carried and deposited by water, but was instead on a mountainside where it followed quartz veins deep into the earth. It was a simple problem with a simple solution. Dig. What these gold seekers didn't fathom was that the holes they started in 1850 would deepen over the next 106 years to 11,000 feet on the incline, reaching more than a mile below the surface. When the Empire finally closed in 1956, the solid granite bedrock below was honeycombed with 367 miles of tunnels.

But how was George Roberts to know all that? He couldn't resist when a buyer waved $350 in his face in 1851. He sold his mine thinking he'd gotten the better deal. But by 1864, with the central shaft inching deeper every day, the Empire—as it was then called—had yielded over $1 million in gold.

The town of Grass Valley popped up next to the mine. Where a handful of people had lived in 1850, there were 20,000 in 1851. Argonauts arrived from near and far. The most valued of these were the men from Cornwall, reputed to be the best hard-rock miners in the world. For a thousand years their people had mined copper and tin on the Cornish peninsula of southwest England. It became immediately apparent to the Californians that these Cornish blokes knew what they were doing. They brought with them high morale, good humor, an unbreachable fraternity, and a shining work ethic as resistant to corrosion as the metal they mined. And they brought their families. Eventually the Cornish became 85 percent of Grass Valley's population and 90 percent of the Empire's work force. With their keen abilities to follow twisted veins of gold-bearing quartz, with their "Cornish plunging pumps" that raised 18,000 gallons of water out of the mine per hour, and with their underground "sixth sense" that enabled them to hear, smell, and see what

other miners could not, the Cornish were well worth their $3 per day.

Imagine them sitting down there a half mile below the surface, heating their meat and potato pies (called pasties) over a single candleflame in the damp, half-lit darkness. They always saved a morsel for the rats. Like canaries kept in the coal mines of Appalachia, the rats in the Empire were important indicators of air quality. If there was danger, such as methane from rotting timbers, the dying rats would warn the miners.

More colorful than the rats and the miners, though, were the mules. At one time over 40 mules worked in the Empire Mine. They went down about a year after birth and never came back out. It sounds worse than it was. The mules had clean stalls, fresh food and water every day, plus the attention of a muleskinner and veterinarian when necessary. Even so, they were obstinate and stubborn. A mule might not work until rewarded with a handful of oats or a snuff of tobacco or a shot of whiskey. Or worse yet, it'd demand all three. A miffed mule might stand in a narrow tunnel and bloat out its stomach whenever a miner tried to pass. And if a miner tried to hitch a mule to eight one-ton ore carts, he'd get nowhere. The mules would dutifully pull seven tons of ore but no more, no matter how much oats, snuff, or whiskey was proferred.

The grit-and-grime world of the Empire miners was in sharp contrast to that of their company's owner, William B. Bourn, Jr., who vacationed two to four weeks a year in his 15-room Empire "Cottage" next door. (His true home, the Filoli Mansion—named after his motto "Fight, Love, Live"—is in San Francisco.) Bourn would have stayed longer at the Empire, but he disliked the noise of the stamp mill crushing the ore.

Bourn inherited the Empire Mine from his father in 1877 at the age of 21. Although born with a silver spoon in his mouth, he had the unusual ability to sidestep the trappings of wealth and get

A father and son, top, romp around the sumptuous lawns and fountains at the Empire Cottage. KIM HEACOX

The Chinese drug store, bottom, at Columbia had a fast trade, selling everything from tea to opium to fireworks. KEN McKOWEN

down to the business of making bold, clear-headed decisions.

Bourn was the financial genius behind the Empire Mine, but George Starr was the technical genius. Beginning at age 16 as a mucker (one who clears debris from the tunnels and shafts)—the lowest and toughest job in the mines—he worked his way up in 11 years to mine superintendent. The miners called him the "Shining Starr of the Empire" and the "Mining Genius." Between them Bourn and Starr made the Empire a showcase of mining technology, attracting geologists and engineers from around the world. Time and time again they found ways to push the mine deeper and to keep the company out of red ink. Starr quit for a while and went to the mines of South Africa, but Bourn lured him back with the promise of $200,000, money not for himself but for investments in newer technologies for the Empire.

Thus the working triumvirate—Bourn, Starr, and the Cornish—made the Empire one of the most productive and successful hard-rock gold mines in America. Grief-struck by the death of his daughter, William Bourn sold the Empire to Newmont Corporation in 1929 for only $250,000, less than the value of the stamp mill alone. In 1956 astronomical operating costs finally forced the mine to shut down. Although the Empire's revenues had topped $136 million, gold paid only $35 an ounce while the cost of mining it had climbed

The vestiges of golden days die hard in Bodie. An old fire hydrant reminds us that tinderbox towns built in a month could burn down in a night. Bodie burned more than once (like most gold rush towns) but its citizens dutifully built it up again, even after most of the gold was gone. The buildings have since slumped into the earth from decades of neglect, adding to rather than detracting from the ghost town charm. LARRY ULRICH

to $48 an ounce. Twenty percent of the estimated Empire gold had been removed, enough that if melted down into one pure block it would measure seven cubic feet. Reopening the mine was considered around 1979 when gold rocketed to about $800 an ounce. But considering the equally astronomical costs of mining so deep for it, experts said gold would have to climb to $1,000 an ounce and stabilize there to make operations profitable. Nobody is holding his breath.

The State of California paid over $1 million in 1975 for the surface rights of the Empire, not to mine gold, but history. The value of the park today is priceless.

Bodie State Historic Park

Bad men, bad whiskey, bad weather. Yep, Bodie was bad all right. Murders and robberies and fistfights were as common as the wind and as nasty, too. Six men were shot and killed in one week in 1879. Two others erupted over a card deal and knifed each other to death. Undertaking was a lively business in Bodie. An oilcloth painting of the Ten Commandments entitled *Thou Shalt Not Steal* hung in the Methodist Church until, that's right, it was stolen.

"There is some irresistible power that impels us to cut and shoot each other to pieces," wrote the editor of one of Bodie's four newspapers. The Reverend F.M. Warrington had stronger words, denouncing Bodie as "a sea of sin lashed by tempests of lust and passion."

Even the girls were bad. Lottie Johl, Rosa May, and Madame Moustache (who refused to kiss any man with hair on his face) ran the brothels on backstreets misnamed Maiden Lane and Virgin Alley.

Winters settled down like iron, cold enough to make one's teeth ache. Temperatures dropped to -40°F, winds blew 60 miles per hour, and snow drifted 20 feet high. "The worst climate out of doors," someone said. No wonder a small child whose family was about to move there prayed,

"Goodbye, God, we're going to Bodie."

The scent of sage still wafts through Bodie, high in the desert of the Great Basin off the northeast flank of the Sierra Nevada.

The wind still howls, and the coyotes do, too, lending a lonely authenticity to the place. Only powerlines and a parking lot detract from the unvarnished ghost-town atmosphere and remind us of the century to which we belong. The wild days are gone, but not the evidence. Bodie's filled with stories and with the sounds of shouting and shooting, horses and stagecoaches, music and laughter. It echoes with the swinging of saloon doors, the clinking of shot glasses, the heavy jingling of money bags, and the secret intonement of the makeshift prayers endemic to any town demented by gold. With patience and imagination one can hear it all in the streets of Bodie.

Throughout the 1850s men scoured the high country of California in search of gold, nursing the forlorn hope that any day they'd find the mother lode—a pocket of riches greater than anything yet found. In 1859 a small group of prospectors discovered placer deposits in the desert northeast of Mono Lake. A tent town popped up immediately. Among the prospectors was William S. Body, a Dutchman from New York. Winter came early that year, trapping Body and his partner, E.S. Taylor, in a snowy whiteout somewhere between Mono Lake and their camp. Taylor survived, but all he found of Body the next spring was some bones picked clean by coyotes and ravens. A sign painter marked the grave "Bodie," and the prospectors adopted the name for their town. It was an inauspicious beginning, yet the circumstances couldn't have been more appropriate for a town destined to become a sink of broken dreams, cold loneliness, and untimely death.

Bodie grew slowly at first. The gold lay hidden in hard-rock deposits in the surrounding hills and it wasn't easy to find. Miners and mining experts down on their luck came to Bodie to try their skills,

A park maintenance man finishes a new roof on one of the 170 buildings still standing at Bodie State Historic Park, near Mono Lake on the east side of the Sierra Nevada. WILLIAM HELSEL

but the next ten years yielded only frustration. A little gold here, a little gold there—just enough to drive a man crazy.

Finally, in 1875 the nearby Bunker Hill claim was discovered and Bodie snapped out of its torpor. This was to be the last hurrah for many California argonauts, and they poured into the town like bees to honey. Tides of riffraff followed, and by 1878 Bodie boasted 6,000 to 10,000 residents, 600 buildings (170 are still standing), and a mile-long main street filled with color and character.

Most of the miners were Cornish while the shopkeepers, craftsmen, and laborers were Italians, Irish, Germans, and Jews. A few Chinese ran their opium dens and gambling houses, but most peddled fruits and vegetables. And it was the Chinese who hauled in and sold most of the firewood.

The fluted, eroded cliffs at Malakoff Diggins State Historic Park are reflected in a foreground tailing pond long since abandoned by miners. By washing away large amounts of earth with hydraulic hoses, it became profitable to mine gravel here that yielded less than a nickel's worth of gold per cubic yard. BRIAN R. BROWN

For Bodie, above timberline at 8,500 feet in the desert, wood was precious. Hooligans constantly stole firewood from homes until the owners devised a plan. They drilled a hole in the wood,

filled it with blasting powder, sealed it, and put it back on the pile. After a few surprise explosions, the wood thefts stopped.

Next to gold, beer was Bodie's main export. Three to seven breweries and about 65 saloons kept things flowing. "If you have anything to drink in a bottle, pass it around," read the Bodie stagecoach rules. "In very cold weather abstain entirely from liquor...because you will freeze twice as quickly when under its influence...Don't point out where murders have been committed if there are any women passengers....Expect annoyances, discomforts, and some hardships." The stage from San Francisco took 30 hours.

Bodie wasn't all bad. Like any other town it had its respectable neighborhood. A group known as Citizens Committee 601 was organized to clean things up. Outlaws had 24 hours to get out of town, or else they'd end up in a shallow grave on Boot Hill. One has to wonder if in fighting fire with fire the Citizens Committee 601 reduced the violence or added to it.

By 1882 the life and the gold was ebbing out of Bodie. The days of $400,000 of bullion per month were gone. Gold strikes in Arizona and Idaho further emptied Bodie's streets. Fires gutted the town in 1892 and 1932, but many of the structures were rebuilt. Still standing is the town jail, Bodie Bank, Masonic House, firehouse, Boone Store and Warehouse, schoolhouse, Miner's Union Hall, and many other buildings and homes.

Bottles line the shelves and tumbleweeds blow across the streets. Cobwebs veil the windows and old doors creak in the wind. Picket fences wrap around the broken porches of gaunt, ghostly buildings. Coyotes trot through the dust and ravens land on the gabled rooftops. Bodie belongs to them now.

The California gold rush lasted only a couple of decades, but the aftermath lingered on much longer. Obsessed, argonauts spread throughout the

foothills and mountains of California to poke their picks at the slightest provocation of gold. The hardy times of the goldseekers are commemorated in three other parks: Shasta, Plumas-Eureka, and Malakoff Diggins.

It made good sense to Pierson B. Reading, after seeing the Coloma Valley where James Marshall had discovered gold, that his land being of similar geography should also hold riches. Sure enough it did. His secret lasted as long as his patience. In just a couple years up popped Shasta City, the "Queen City of the Northern Mines." It was a typical boom-and-bust tinderbox town, and like most others was filled with boisterous ballyhoo, foreign languages, and domestic squabbles.

But Shasta City fell into a slow, steady decline as it was bypassed by wagon roads and railroads. Extensive restoration at Shasta State Historic Park has preserved many of the buildings, such as the courthouse, the Litsch Store, the Masonic Hall, and the Pioneer Barn.

Called the "most scenic of California's gold districts," Plumas-Eureka State Park sits on the high and remote east slope of the Sierra Nevada, 80 miles north of Lake Tahoe. The old town of Johnsville and the Plumas-Eureka stamp mills tell their stories, but many visitors become more absorbed in the surrounding scenery. The camping is excellent and the hiking is even better.

Malakoff Diggins State Historic Park is the site of one of the largest hydraulic gold mines in the world. The great hydraulic hoses are gone now, but not the evidence of their use. This type of mining literally moved mountains and ravaged valleys. Eight-inch nozzles blasted the cliffs with a spray "strong enough to kill a man." Each day 60 million gallons of water washed away 50 thousand tons of gravel, leaving behind the heavy deposits of gold. The erosion was phenomenal, and a disgruntled John Muir wrote, "Man will be shown counting his wealth in terms of bits of paper representing other bits of scarce but

The streamside ingenuity of the gold seeker

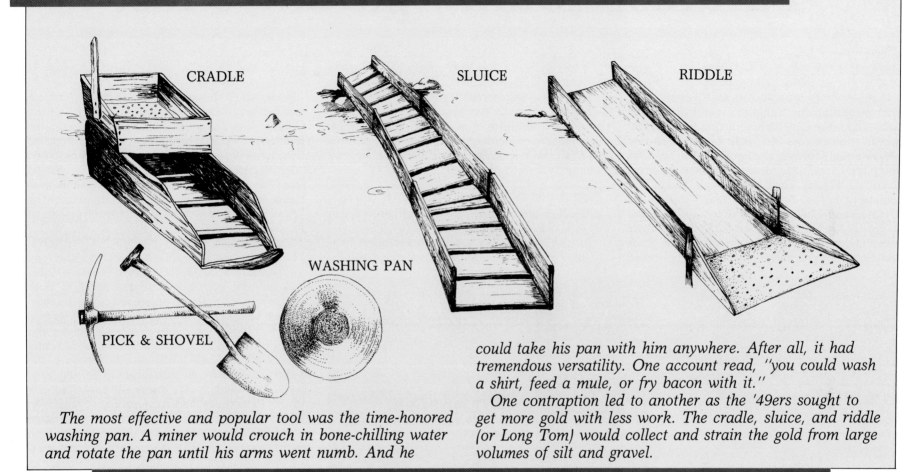

CRADLE

SLUICE

RIDDLE

WASHING PAN

PICK & SHOVEL

The most effective and popular tool was the time-honored washing pan. A miner would crouch in bone-chilling water and rotate the pan until his arms went numb. And he could take his pan with him anywhere. After all, it had tremendous versatility. One account read, "you could wash a shirt, feed a mule, or fry bacon with it."

One contraption led to another as the '49ers sought to get more gold with less work. The cradle, sluice, and riddle (or Long Tom) would collect and strain the gold from large volumes of silt and gravel.

comparatively useless metal that are kept buried in strong vaults. Meanwhile, the soil, the only real wealth that can keep mankind alive on the face of this earth, is savagely being cut loose from its ancient moorings and washed into the seven seas." Public trust laws invoked by the California Supreme Court eventually halted hydraulic mining at Malakoff Diggins.

Gold fever never dies, it just goes into remission and flares up again. It leaves behind a wild, half-crazy, seldom-dull legacy that provides endless entertainment and intrigue. Who can walk those historical streets and valleys today without feeling the slightest twinge of gold fever? Maybe there's a nugget around here somewhere. ■

Paradise found, paradise lost

Prophets and propagandists said there was no finer place on earth. California was the promised land. The same enlightenment that had brought the Pilgrims across the Atlantic now carried American settlers over the Great Plains, Russians down the Canada and Oregon coasts, and Asians across the Pacific. They were people looking for something better. The "Great Itch," they called it—the overwhelming urge to go to California. For some, like the ill-fated Donner Party, getting there was a nightmare. Others found a paradise. Some had designs on great wealth; some merely wanted a new home with fertile land and freedom.

Dozens of parks commemorate the pioneers who stood at historic crossroads and by their strengths, weaknesses, successes, and failures made the California State Park System a story of people as well as of scenery.

Fort Ross State Historic Park

The Russians were in California and the Spanish were shocked.

In the summer of 1812 Commander Ivan Kuskov and a crew of 94 Russians and 40 Aleut Indians sailed down the coast of North America and landed in California, 100 miles north of the Golden Gate. Before the Spanish noticed them, the Russians had built a village and a sturdy fort called Ross (after Rossiya, or Russia) and had mounted 20 to 40 cannon. One request after another arrived from the presidio in San Francisco asking them to leave, but they politely ignored them all. The Spanish were powerless to evict the Russians at Ross and both sides knew it.

The Russians weren't here to make trouble. They had come to hunt sea otters, to grow food for themselves and for their parent colony in Sitka, and to establish trade with the Spanish. Both settlements could have prospered from commercial exchange, but the monarchy in Madrid had long forbidden trade between her colonies and foreigners. And even though Spain was currently allied with Russia in a war against Napoleon, she nevertheless adhered stubbornly to her outdated laws. The alliance was uneasy at best. The czar in St. Petersburg had expansionist designs on North America and like any other imperialist couldn't be trusted beyond arm's length. But both St. Petersburg and Madrid were too preoccupied by wars and infighting to concern themselves seriously with this place called California. So Fort Ross and El Presidio de San Francisco, the most distant outposts of two mismanaged empires, existed side by side in mutual, friendly tolerance.

A familiar winter fog veils the morning sun as it rises behind a Fremont cottonwood, a common resident of the state park units in the Central Valley. In summer, pioneers found welcome shade beneath these large trees that take their name from John Charles Frémont, an important explorer in California in the 1840s and a candidate for the U.S. presidency in 1856.
D. CAVAGNARO

In 1833 a young officer named Mariano Guadalupe Vallejo, the same man who later established Petaluma Adobe and founded the towns Sonoma and Santa Rosa, was dispatched by Governor Jose Figueroa to assess the Russians' strength at Ross. Graciously received, Vallejo noted a shipyard, an armory, and multiple gun emplacements—all very impressive—and 800 cattle, 700 horses, 2,000 sheep, 400 fruit trees, 700 vines, and 300 people (70 Russians, the rest Aleuts and California Indians). But only six years later, with the sea otter populations decimated, the Russians were ready to leave. They sold their fort and holdings for a small down payment to John Sutter in 1841. In some respects the Californios were sorry to see them go. It wasn't the Russians that concerned them now, it was the Americans.

Nearly a century and a half later, Fort Ross still evokes the flavor and spirit the Russians brought to California. Many buildings were destroyed in the great 1906 earthquake and have since been rebuilt. But probably the most significant outpouring of affection for Fort Ross occurred after the old Russian Orthodox chapel burned to the ground in 1970. The original bell, which the fire had melted, was recast in Belgium. And with funds raised through state, private, and corporate channels, the chapel was reconstructed and dedicated before a cheering crowd in June 1974.

Sutter's Fort and Old Sacramento State Historic Parks

The pre-1850 history of Sacramento revolves largely around one man: Captain John Sutter.

But let's get a few things straight from the start. He was born Johann August Suter in Switzerland

A supply room in Fort Ross depicts the pioneer lives of the Russians who lived in California from 1812 to 1841. Much of the old fort was destroyed in the great 1906 earthquake and has since been restored, like this room, to convincing perfection.
JAMES M. HARRIS

in 1803 and came to America, one historian noted, "as a fugitive from tragedy and justice." On the verge of being thrown into a Swiss debtor's prison in 1834 for the failure of his dry goods business, he deserted his wife and five children and sailed to America. Although he claimed to be a former captain of the "Royal Swiss Guard of France," the rank was nothing more than a wild concoction of Sutter's fertile imagination.

After wayfaring from St. Louis to Santa Fe to Oregon to Honolulu to Sitka, Sutter finally arrived in Monterey, the provincial capital of Mexican California, in July 1839. His timing was perfect. The Mexican governor, embroiled in a turf war with officials up north (primarily Mariano Vallejo in Sonoma), felt he could use Sutter to strengthen his advantage and immediately bestowed upon the Swiss immigrant 50,000 acres—the largest land grant available—in the Great Central Valley at the confluence of the Sacramento and American rivers. It was Sutter's dream come true; a chance to develop his own settlement. He would call it "New Helvetia" (New Switzerland), and he intended to run it like a European principality.

Using Indians as serf labor, Sutter sold beaver pelts and wild-grape brandy and soon expanded into farming and cattle ranching. With credit that looked much better than it was, he purchased livestock, tools, and cannon from the Russians departing Fort Ross in 1841. Earlier that year survivors of the first American wagon train to cross the Sierra Nevada had arrived at the simple adobe fort Sutter had built on a hill about a mile east of the Sacramento River. Sutter's Fort, people called it, and they put it on the map at the end of the California Trail.

For the next decade Sutter's Fort was a mecca for tens of thousands of wagon-weary settlers. And there to greet them would be John Sutter, locally known as the "Good Captain" or the "honorable proprietor," always generous yet always out to make a sale. His fort bustled with optimism and

Sheep and cattle still occupy the stock pens at Sutter's Fort, top, and bridles and harnesses hang on the walls. KIM HEACOX

A woman fits and stitches clothing for a young boy, bottom, during Living History Day, when park aides, volunteers, and rangers portray Indian and pioneer life at Sutter's Fort in the 1840s. KEN McKOWEN

a commercial blend of weavers, coopers, carpenters, spinners, and hatters, all sharing stories from the trail or ambitions for the future.

A stormy political climate blew into northern California in 1846. At Sutter's Fort the Mexican flag was replaced by the rebellious Bear Flag, which in turn was replaced by the Stars and Stripes. By 1847 California belonged to the United States, and the fort was a U.S. military post. New Helvetia, having been founded on a Mexican land grant, was largely dissolved. Sutter suddenly found himself without a barony, although he did manage to retain some of his land and livestock.

With one more scheme up his sleeve, Sutter decided to build a sawmill on the American River in the Sierra foothills and from there float milled lumber down to the Central Valley and sell it for premium prices. Imagine his shock when his partner, James Marshall, arrived from the mill with a pocket full of gold dust. Sutter tried to keep it quiet, but keeping gold a secret then was like trying to hold back the sea. Word leaked out and by the summer of 1848 California was delirious with gold fever. Sutter watched in agony as his fort, his cattle, and his horses were abandoned by workers headed for the hills. It's odd that Sutter, who had capitalized many times on being in the right place at the right time, would miss this greatest of opportunities. Instead of raking in a fortune, he fumbled from one futile enterprise to another and finally disappeared into the flood of 100,000 gold seekers.

Sutter's Fort was dying while Sacramento grew like a weed on the banks of its namesake river. Where in November 1848 not a single house had stood, a year later was a hive of shanties, tents, and wagons filled with 12,000 argonauts. They were rugged men who had crossed America for gold and had arrived here, in Sacramento, to buy picks, shovels, beans, and whiskey.

The town was on land formerly of Sutter's New Helvetia, and lively talk ensued as to whether the new arrivals were settlers or squatters.

Things came to a boil in the summer of 1850 when a "squatters riot" killed a dozen men, including the sheriff and the city assessor, and wounded the mayor. Law and order prevailed, however, and despite several serious fires, Sacramento became the state capital in 1854 and grew thereafter at a steady, healthy rate.

Sutter's Fort and Old Sacramento are alive and well today. Both have been restored (in facade, at least) to look much as they did in 1846. To step into Sutter's Fort during a living history demonstration is to find women cooking pioneer meals over open fires and John Sutter himself to welcome "new-come settlers."

Seventy-five shops, stores, museums, hotels, and historical points of interest await the visitor at Old Sacramento. History buffs will find 14 buildings and monuments that rekindle bygone days. The B.F. Hastings Building was the western terminus for the famous Pony Express and for Western Union's transcontinental telegraph line. The second floor housed the State Supreme Court and has been restored to impeccable authenticity. The bottom floor has been converted into a communications museum.

Although Sacramento was born on gold, it was raised on railroads. California's "Big Four"—Leland Stanford, Mark Hopkins, Collis Huntington, and Charles Crocker—joined efforts here to

Front Street is seldom this quiet at Old Sacramento. Over one million visitors a year discover the shops, museums, and restaurants at this popular state historic park sandwiched between Interstate 5 and the Sacramento River.
GEORGE WUERTHNER

plan and spearhead the U.S. Transcontinental Railroad. Construction began in 1863 with the Central Pacific Line moving east from Sacramento and the Union Pacific Line moving west from Omaha. The dreams bore fruit six years later at the driving of the Golden Spike in Promontory, Utah. America was bridged coast to coast by railroad. The trip that had taken six months by wagon in 1849 took two weeks by train in 1869. Sacramento bustled with top-hatted Easterners who stepped off trains at the Central Pacific Railroad Passenger Station and could hardly believe they were in California.

The Big Four Building, Huntington & Hopkins Hardware, and the Central Pacific Railroad Passenger Station still evoke a heady feeling that the formative days of railroading in America were only yesterday. But by far the single most popular site in Old Sacramento is the handsome, spacious Railroad Museum. Billed as the finest of its kind in North America, the 100,000-square-foot museum displays over 20 restored locomotives and cars dating from the 29-foot steampowered Huntington built in 1863 to the 126-foot SP Cubforward of 1944. The Virginia & Truckee Locomotive 21 was built in 1875 to haul gold and lumber and was later featured in the 1939 Cecil B. DeMille film, *Union Pacific*. Visitors can enter

Hyacinthe sleeping car to feel the 1929 "regal restfulness" of improved night train travel. And a daily movie gives a good overview of the museum and of the history of railroads in America. There are even volunteers dressed in engineer's garb who stroll about and answer questions. "If you're not a train nut when you come into this place," a man remarked, "you will be when you come out."

Donner Memorial State Park

This was paradise lost. No single experience among nineteenth-century American pioneers exceeded the tragedy of the Donner Party. Eighty-one people attempted to cross the Sierra Nevada in late October 1846; only 47 survived. Trapped by severe cold and heavy winter snows, they exhausted their food, they lost their wits and senses, and they did the unthinkable. The living ate the dead.

History has since treated the Donner tragedy with both compassion and contempt. Some critics say it could have happened to anyone; some say George Donner, the party leader, was a bumbling megalomaniac; some say westering pioneers were masters of their own fate and that the Donner Party had no one to blame but themselves. John Muir quipped afterwards that they could have

enjoyed their winter had they known how to live off the land.

The problems began early. They took the untested Hastings Cutoff out of Fort Bridger and lost more time than they saved. They tarried too long in Nevada, underestimating the seriousness of California's mountains.

And they hit an unusually hard winter. When a relief party finally reached them with packs full of food, an emaciated woman staggered out of the snow and cried, "Are you from California or Heaven?" Be it bad luck or bad judgement, the Donner tragedy burned like a hot iron into the psyche of American pioneers. Years later one only had to whisper "Donner" to keep the wagons moving.

Traffic on Interstate 80 today zips over Donner Pass in stark contrast to the predicament of 1846. Families stop to picnic and to walk the nature trail, or to crosscountry ski and build snowmen. Teachers hold workshops here. Every so often someone lays a wreath of flowers at the memorial. Mothers and fathers try to explain to their children what happened here a long, long time ago, and why. It isn't easy.

Colonel Allensworth State Historic Park

This is a story that every child in America should hear.

Born a slave in Louisville, Kentucky, in 1842, Allen Allensworth was "sold down the river" at age 15 when he was caught attempting to learn to read and write, skills prohibited to blacks in the South. He ran away but was caught, sold again, and eventually shipped to New Orleans and thrown into a "nigger pen" with a thousand other slaves. Trapped in a sorry, fetid world of human injustice, young Allensworth began to develop the rock-hard resolve that would bring him to California and to a life and promise then unimagined by blacks. The American dream would be his dream.

He escaped to the North and joined the U.S. Navy, rising to the rank of first class petty officer during the Civil War. Buoyed by an honorable discharge and a brief but successful restaurant business in St. Louis, he was ordained a Baptist minister in 1871. Ten years later Allensworth entered American history books when he joined the U.S. Army and President Grover Cleveland appointed him the first black chaplain. He served throughout the United States and Indian territories, participated in the Spanish-American War and the Philippine liberation, and retired in 1906 as a lieutenant colonel, then the highest rank ever held by a black American in the United States armed services.

The plight of blacks—the insults, injuries, and injustices they endured or could not endure— prompted Allensworth to search for a community where blacks could become economically, socially, culturally, and politically self-sufficient. He wanted a new land for new lives. He gathered his wife and two children, packed his bags, and moved to California. While searching in the San Joaquin Valley, the colonel found a fertile, relatively inexpensive plot of land about 30 miles north of Bakersfield. The surface water looked good, and the groundwater table was high. Thus, on August 3, 1908, one man's dream for his people became a reality. The *Tulare Register* announced, "The town, which is to be called Allensworth, is

to enable colored people to live on in equity with whites and to encourage industry and thrift in the race." It was the first and only town in California founded, financed, and governed by black Americans.

Although California had joined the Union as a free state, subsequent laws effectively eroded the rights of blacks. Schools and other public facilities were segregated. Voting rights were denied. And no black could testify against any white.

But Allensworth was another world. One account described it as "offering its inhabitants the chance to participate fully in a community, to practice high ideals and principles, to make and enforce their own laws, to own property, and to seek and reach their individual and collective goals." It's little wonder why blacks from across the state—artisans, craftsmen, farmers, ranchers, businessmen, and others—moved to a brighter future at Allensworth.

The town prospered at first with the cultivation of grain, cotton, alfalfa, sugar beets, dairy cattle, chickens, turkeys, and hares. There were several stores, a bakery, drug store, livery stable, barber shop, and machine shop—35 buildings in all. Most impressive were the school, library, and the Allensworth Hotel. Hard times befell the town when long, costly legal battles over water rights (with white-owned companies) slowly strangled agricultural productivity. Many residents left in the twenties and thirties, others went to war in the forties and fifties, but a few remained behind to work the fields. Finally, in 1966 dangerous amounts of arsenic were found in the drinking

Colonel Allen Allensworth, born a slave in Louisville, Kentucky, in 1842. PHOTO COURTESY CALIFORNIA DEPARTMENT OF PARKS AND RECREATION

to commemorate the rock-hard resolve to live a free life—a resolve that began 130 years ago in the mind of a runaway slave.

Angel Island State Park

If the West Coast had an Ellis Island, it would be Angel Island, anchored in the middle of San Francisco Bay and in the memories of thousands of immigrants and U.S. troops.

Beginning in the 1860s, Camp Reynolds (at West Garrison) was a duty station for Union soldiers during the Civil War. Later, the huge "Welcome" signs at Fort McDowell (at East Garrison) greeted battle-weary soldiers coming home from the Pacific at the end of World War II. For many years the fort was the nation's only overseas processing station. Forty thousand troops a year passed through Angel Island. German and Japanese Americans were detained here periodically during the wars. And immigrants from Asia and Latin America set first foot on United States soil on Angel Island. It was a place for tears of joy and for tears of sorrow.

A Nike missile base, launching site, and radar control station operated here in the fifties and sixties, after which the state began its piecemeal acquisition of park land.

Angel Island could just as easily be in "The Incomparable Coast" chapter, given its tremendous scenic beauty. The two-mile-long Cove-to-Crest Nature Trail climbs 781 feet from Ayala Cove to the top of Mount Caroline Livermore for a panoramic view of Marin County, the Golden Gate Bridge, and the entire San Francisco Bay Area. Blends of grassland, brushland, and forest host a wide variety of plants, animals, and birds.

Aspects of Angel Island still evoke the flavor of the times before the white man came when the Coast Miwoks paddled their tule canoes and hunted seal, deer, quail, and waterfowl. What must they have thought when Lieutenant Juan Manuel de Ayala sailed the Spanish galleon *San Carlos* into San Francisco Bay in August 1775. It was the first sailing ship to enter one of the greatest natural harbors in the world. Ayala anchored in the cove that bears his name and immediately claimed the great bay for Spain. For San Francisco Bay and its Coast Miwoks, things would never be the same. A paradise had been found and paradise had been lost.

Fort Humboldt and Fort Tejon State Historic Parks

"How foresaken I feel here," a soldier stationed at Fort Humboldt (in the present-day town of Eureka) penned to his wife in 1854. "Whoever hears of me in ten years will hear of a well-to-do Missouri farmer." Not hardly. That depressed soldier was Ulysses S. Grant. In ten years he was commanding general of the Union's Army of the Potomac and shortly thereafter became president of the United States. Fifteen officers who served at Fort Tejon (36 miles south of Bakersfield) also became generals in the American Civil War, eight with the Union and seven with the Confederacy.

California was not the most enviable assignment in the military. Supplies, mail, and paychecks seldom arrived on time. There was adventure, but soldiers battled boredom more than Indians.

Forts Humboldt and Tejon were established in the early 1850s to thwart Indian uprisings in the wake of greedy land-grabbing by white settlers. Horse theft and cattle rustling had to be stopped. Peacekeeping patrols out of Fort Humboldt rode up and down the coast and east into the unpredictable Modoc country, while those from Fort Tejon explored the Owens Valley, protected supply routes to Los Angeles, and traveled as far as Salt Lake City. The forts became social and political centers where settlers found comforting signs of civilization; the Stars and Stripes reminded them that California truly did belong to the United States.

Each fort commanded a beautiful view:

water. With most of its people gone and the buildings in shambles, Allensworth looked doomed.

A few years later several historical societies recognized Allensworth as an area of statewide historical significance. A half-million dollars was allocated by state senate and assembly bills, and in 1974 the State Park and Recreation Commission created Colonel Allensworth State Historic Park

Framed between blossoms of pride of Madeira in the foreground and the ramparts of San Francisco in the background, West Garrison and Camp Reynolds stand on the shore of Angel Island where soldiers once arrived for duty during the Civil War. FRANK S. BALTHIS

Weaverville Joss House State Historic Park

Who were these people? In 1847 they numbered no more than 100 in all California, but a few years later over 20,000 were at the gold diggings. They clung stubbornly to homeland customs, wore floppy shirts and wide straw hats, drank boiled tea instead of doubtful ditchwater, and in sharp contrast to the hard-gambling and heavy-drinking whites, they played low-stake card games and preferred opium to alcohol. They wore their hair in long braided pigtails, called queues, which Americans insisted they cut off to qualify for residence in California. They were frugal, industrious, and honest people, yet they were hated.

They were Chinese. And Weaverville Joss House (in Weaverville, 50 miles west of Redding) was a place of worship. Touted as the "oldest continuously used Chinese temple in California," the original structure burned to the ground in 1873 and was rebuilt two years later. Inside, before the images of the gods of Health, Decision, and Mercy, Chinese pray today to attain harmony with nature through the Tao—"the Way"—an ancient form of worship infused with elements of Confucianism and Buddhism. They can ask for purity and simplicity in their everyday lives, but never for wealth or revenge. Kneeling before the ornately carved altar, they offer candles, incense, food, and money. Inside and out, the structures are painted bright red, a Taoist symbol of happiness.

The Chinese had good reason to come to California. Famine and political upheaval had paralyzed their country for a decade, and many

Humboldt on a 40-foot bluff east of Humboldt Bay and Tejon at the mouth of an important pass in the Tehachapi Mountains. One visitor wrote, "The post of Tejon is on a little plain, entirely surrounded by high mountains, beautifully situated in a grove of old oaks; at this season [spring] the fort is most romantic and beautiful. The noble oaks are in full leaf....An oasis in the desert where all is freshness and life."

Although only a few of the 20 original Fort Tejon buildings remain standing, one can sense the military air of the time when cavalry men lined up for inspection in their hot wool uniforms or of the time when the famous Camel Corps arrived after surveying a wagon road from New Mexico. The fort slumbers in a reverie of days gone by until living history demonstrations and Civil War skirmishes fill the air with ballyhoo and gunfire. Suddenly the year is 1861 and Fort Tejon is very much alive.

At Fort Humboldt a self-guiding trail winds through displays of northern California military and logging history. Visitors can begin at a handsome museum and proceed to an authentic logger's cabin and to the park's main attraction, the Falk and Andersonia Gypsy locomotives that once hauled huge redwood and Douglas fir logs to the mill.

The ornately carved altar of Weaverville Joss House, the oldest continuously used Chinese temple in California, bathes in a glow of red light, a Taoist expression of happiness. The wooden canopies of gods along the back wall are fronted by candles, incense sticks, oracle fortune sticks, and wine cups. FRANK S. BALTHIS

dutifully sent their earnings back to wives and children across the Pacific. Historian William Weber Johnson writes that "they would work abandoned claims and tailings for specks of gold white men considered unworthy of the effort. The worst possible digging was described as one that 'even the Chinese passed by.' And on the rare occasions when the Chinese miners turned up a promising prospect, they were driven off by the white men."

But no chapter in California history highlights the physical and spiritual endurance of the Chinese more than the building of the railroads. When the volatile Irish threatened to strike, it was the Chinese who replaced them. One account says they were "quick to learn, slow to complain, and ready to start work when the whistle blew...they were not inclined to strike, did not get drunk on payday, did not frequent the whorehouses...and did not lean on the pick handle when the boss was not looking." But they did have "an outrageous

habit of bathing everyday." No other people laid more steel rails in California in the 1860s, and it was a crew of tough but humble Chinese who ceremoniously put the last rail of the Transcontinental Railroad in place.

They called California *Kum Saan*—the "Gold Mountain"—an opportunity for peace and prosperity. They brought new hopes, old customs, and even older spiritual beliefs. Today, more than 5 percent of California's 26 million people are Asian Americans. The Weaverville Joss House, then, is more than a religious shrine; it is a small but ornate window into a people who bent their backs and calloused their hands to make California what it is today.

California always promised something better: bluer skies, greener pastures, golden shores, and brighter futures. Folks back East used to say, "If hell lay to the West, Americans would cross heaven to get there." Ensconced in his New

England woods, Henry David Thoreau wrote, "Eastward I go by force, but westward I go free...the prevailing tendency of my countrymen." It's not easy to promise paradise and live up to it, but California did and for many still does.

Several other state parks—Bale Grist Mill, Benicia Capitol, China Camp, Railtown 1897, and Wassama Round House—commemorate California's history, as do the parks in the chapters: "The Early Ones," "The Californios," "Gold Fever," and "Famous Homes." Immigrants came and many stayed by choice, filling the land with barely believable stories of paradise found and paradise lost—stories preserved today in the state park system. ■

A California sister butterfly alights on a poppy. Because of the diverse terrain encompassed by the California State Park System, an equally diverse community of organisms—plants, insects, fish, amphibians, reptiles, birds, and mammals—can find at least some protection. D. CAVAGNARO

Famous homes

To come from nowhere, rise to fame, make a fortune, and build a dream house is the ultimate expression of success in America. This chapter and the parks herein commemorate some of the now famous people who did just that and who did it with a dash of California panache. Their dream homes range from a castle to a ranch and from a fortress to a farm. Each mirrors the men and women who made it, and each has been given as a generous gift to the people of California.

Hearst San Simeon State Historical Monument

People say William Randolph Hearst built his castle with his money and influence. But it took more than that—Hearst had imagination.

He took a hill at San Simeon on the California Coast and created a castle fit for a king. The Tudors of England, the Pharaohs of Egypt, and the de' Medicis of Renaissance Italy would feel at home here. Prized chandeliers hang from the ceilings and priceless paintings on the walls. Each spacious room is a step through time and culture, from medieval Gothic (a favorite of Hearst's) to Baroque to contemporary. Each motif blends comfortably into another, creating what Hearst called "the harmonious whole." Even the landscaping is regal as it wraps an emerald cloak around the white outer walls and red tile roofs. Although on California soil, Hearst's castle—his American Dream—is essentially European. Visitors today enjoy the majestic opulence that a few decades ago only Hearst, his family, and his honored guests enjoyed. W.A. Swanberg, Hearst's biographer, notes that Hollywood in the twenties and thirties was divided into two castes: "people who had been guests at San Simeon and those who had not." Among the upper caste were Mary Pickford, Douglas Fairbanks, Greta Garbo, Rudolph Valentino, and Louis Mayer (of Metro-Goldwyn-Mayer). Hearst called them his "wild movie people." What extravagant, exciting times those must have been.

William Randolph Hearst was a young boy hanging onto the tail of a runaway pony when he first ascended that 1,600-foot hill. Growing up in the wild heart of San Simeon was a watershed for him; no place could have better tilled his fertile mind and predisposed him to greatness. His early imagination was probably already brimming with what writer Taylor Coffman calls a "DeMille-like pageant of fable and history."

Perched on a hill like a castle in Bavaria, the home of the newspaper magnate William Randolph Hearst surveys the coast of California at San Simeon, 30 miles northwest of Morro Bay. One of the most famous landmarks in California, Hearst Castle was donated to the state park system in 1958. FRED LYON

It took ten years to complete the Neptune Pool, top, to Hearst's satisfaction. Many guests at San Simeon had a pleasant surprise when they went swimming here. Not only did the pool look divine, it felt divine as well. Hearst filled it with heated water. WILLIAM HELSEL

Dressed with Flemish tapestries and Spanish choir stalls, the Gothic Suite, bottom, was a favorite of William Randolph Hearst. The long central table seated 22 honored guests, and there was ample room to add a second table when needed. GEORGE ELICH

Many years later, during World War I, after his pragmatic, no-nonsense determination had built an empire in the newspaper business, Hearst returned to vacation with his wife and children at San Simeon and wrote to his mother, "We are back in our regular camp at the top of the hill now, tired and sleepy on account of those kids. I love this ranch. It is wonderful. I love the sea, and I love the mountains and the hollows in the hills, and the shady places in the creeks, and the fine old oaks, and even the hot brushy hillsides—full of quail, and the canyons full of deer. I would rather spend a month here than any place in the world. And as a sanitarium! Mother, it has Nauheim, Karlsbad, Vichy, Wiesbaden, French Lick, Saratoga, and every other so-called health resort beat a nautical mile." Hearst had seen the finest retreats in the world—from casas to châteaus to castles—and he knew he could do better. He was ready to come home.

Hearst broke ground in February 1920. A year earlier he had contacted Julia Morgan in San Francisco with the simple confession that he wanted something "more comfortable" at San Simeon. "I get tired of going up there and camping in tents," he told her, "I'm getting a little old for that."

Morgan, described as "easily the most accomplished woman in American architecture," would match Hearst's genius with her own, building and blending for him a fabulous California barony. Hearst called it his "ranch." And he named the site "La Cuesta Encantada," The Enchanted Hill. Artwork and materials poured in from around the world—Persian tiles, Moorish columns, Flemish tapestries, Veronese marble, French Gothic doors, Byzantine courtyard fonts, and Italian Renaissance choir stalls.

Nothing was too extravagant.

For 30 glorious years William Randolph Hearst lived off and on in sumptuous style at San Simeon until his death at age 88 in 1951. "The time to retire is when God retires you," he said, "and not

The ruins of Wolf House, a writer's dream that went up in flames in 1913, is one of several sites visitors can enjoy at the 800-acre Jack London State Historic Park, near Glen Ellen. Trails wind past London's cottage, his grave site, winery ruins, and silos, and eventually lead up the side of Sonoma Mountain amid a mixed forest of madrone, mazanita, redwood, and Douglas fir. ED COOPER

before.'' Hearst never regarded San Simeon as finished. There were always improvements to be made. That was part of the beauty of the place. It kept him alive; it kept him young. He was still that dreamer of a boy holding onto the tail of a runaway pony.

Jack London State Historic Park

Moderation was impossible for Jack London. He lived hard, worked hard, and played hard, grabbing the world by its wild latitudes as he walked the Yukon and sailed the South Pacific. He loved his writing, his whiskey, his wife, and his ranch. Life for London was a brief but unbridled ride out of poverty and into immortality.

"I am the sailor on horseback," he wrote. "Watch my dust! Oh, I shall make mistakes a-many; but watch my dreams come true. Try to dream with me my dreams of fruitful acres. Do not be a slave to an old conception. Try to realize what I am after."

London's dreams came true all right. Reading his books we find a storyteller among the ranks of Poe, Kipling, and Melville. But more than that, more than the undying prose of a brilliant man, there are the dust and the fruitful acres of his Beauty Ranch on the side of Sonoma Mountain near Glen Ellen where one can almost see, hear, and feel the sailor on horseback. Wherever he went, in words or in person, this is the place he came back to. This was home.

"I am putting this ranch into first class shape and am laying a foundation for a good paying industry here," he wrote. "Everything I build is for the years to come." Tragically, those years never came. Weakened by fatigue and chronic illness, London died on November 22, 1916, on the porch at the front of his cottage. He was 40 years old. America was shocked; together with the death of Mark Twain, six years earlier, she had lost her two most popular fictionists.

A virtual museum of one man's memorabilia, Will Rogers' home preserves the life and times of one of America's most beloved humorists. MAXINE CASS

Only a month earlier London had written, "I have no countryside home. I am a farmer. It is because I am a farmer that I live in the country. I am that sort of farmer who, after delving in all the books to satisfy his quest for economic wisdom, returns to the soil as the source and foundation of all economics."

After writing 1,000 words each morning, London would return to the soil to terrace his land, harness his shire horses, or roll up his sleeves to work in his sherry barn. So much was his energy that he even built a piggery with a central feedhouse and 17 separate stalls and dubbed it the "Pig Palace."

Amid the good life and great works there were also discouragements. Probably the most painful was the August night in 1913 when his nearly completed Wolf House burned to the ground. Built on an earthquake-proof foundation for $80,000, it was to last a millennium and be his and his wife

Charmian's dream home.

The loss was a terrible pain, but true to his nature London bounced back with greater vigor than before. Yet perhaps beneath his veneer of gusto and good cheer there lived a sad, dissatisfied man. "Who will reap what I have sown here in this almighty sweet land?" he wrote. "You and I will be forgotten."

That almighty sweet land still lives on the side of Sonoma Mountain. We read your books and watch your dust, Jack London. You're not forgotten.

Will Rogers State Historic Park

Horseman, humorist, writer, and actor, Will Rogers is remembered as "the most beloved man of his generation." Standing on stage in cowboy boots and an Oklahoma grin, he would twirl his rope and lasso his listeners while expounding tongue in cheek on anything from economics to

baseball to unicorns. He was living, lovable proof that the quickest way to America's heart is through her funny bone. "I never met a man I didn't like," he said. Of course not; Will Rogers brought out the best in people.

After circling the world in traveling rodeos and playing with the Ziegfeld Follies in New York, Rogers came to Hollywood in 1919 with a movie offer from Samuel Goldwyn (of Metro-Goldwyn-Mayer).

A few years later the talkies hit the big screen and Rogers' wry country wit shot him to stardom. "Just call me Will," he would say. But the public called him the "Cowboy Philosopher." It was a sad day across America on August 15, 1935, when Will and his friend Wiley Post died in a plane crash in Alaska. He was 55 going on 40, and he left behind not just a grieved nation, but a wife, three children, and a beautiful home in Pacific Palisades, which is now part of the state park that bears his name.

The 31-room Rogers home and 186-acre ranch were donated to the state by Will's wife, Betty, after her death in 1944. The massive fireplace, decorated walls, and homespun memorabilia convey the feeling that Will was here only yesterday. Hiking trails wrap around the corrals, roping arena, and nature center and climb to Inspiration Point. Weekend polo matches continue the traditions of horsemanship and good fun that were so dear to the Cowboy Philosopher.

"You must judge a man's greatness by how much he will be missed," Will said. By his own principle, he was indeed a great man.

Governor's Mansion

Visitors often drive like drunks at the intersection of 16th and H streets in downtown Sacramento. They're turning their heads to look at the Governor's Mansion, a three-story Victorian home crowned with a lofty cupola and ringed by a meticulous botanical garden. But there's no need

Inside the Governor's Mansion, at 16th and H streets in downtown Sacramento, daily tours introduce visitors to the relaxed environment where California's governors lived with their families from 1903 to 1967. CALIFORNIA DEPARTMENT OF PARKS AND RECREATION

to cause an accident; it's better to park and take the 45-minute tour.

When business tycoon Albert Gallatin built the house in 1877, he had no idea that 13 California governors and their families would live there, from George Pardee in 1903 to Ronald Reagan in 1967. The 15-room mansion is a living museum without a stitch of refurbishing or refinishing. It looks no different now than when the Pardee family played and sang at their Steinway piano or when Governor Hiram Johnson lounged on the "plum velvet" sofas after a long day or when Governor Earl Warren (later Chief Justice of the U.S. Supreme Court) wrote at his desk on a typewriter made by San Quentin prison inmates. There are handcrafted bronze hinges and doorknobs, curved mahogany stairs that lead to second-floor bedrooms, elaborate sets of "official State of California china," and gold-framed French mirrors hanging above fireplaces made of Italian marble. The cupola was built in 1879 as a watchtower to track sailing vessels on the Sacramento and American rivers, but the docents who lead tours like to add that "it was also used by one governor as a hideaway to play cards with his cronies."

The mansion cuts away the public veneer of powerful politicians and shows their more intimate, human, and humorous sides. You walk out feeling like you've met them.

William B. Ide Adobe State Historic Park

Thirty-three angry American settlers galloped into Sonoma on June 14, 1846, captured the retired Mexican general, Mariano Guadalupe Vallejo, and claimed themselves a separate "Bear Flag Republic" no longer subject to Mexican rule. But with the impetuous moment behind them, they began to have second thoughts. Would the Mexican Army retaliate and imprison them? They were farmers, after all, not soldiers. As they began to disband, William B. Ide stepped forward and said, "Saddle no horse for me...I will lay my bones here before I will take upon myself the ignominy of commencing an honorable work, and then flee like cowards, like thieves, when no enemy is in sight. In vain will you say you had honorable motives; who will believe it: Flee this day and the longest life cannot wear off your disgrace! Choose ye! Choose ye this day, what you will be! We are robbers, or we must be conquerors!"

The Americans rallied around Ide and elected him their president. But the Bear Flag Republic was short-lived. Twenty-two days later the U.S. Navy captured the Mexican capital at Monterey and the Stars and Stripes was raised over Sonoma.

Ide had arrived in California with his wife and nine children less than a year before the famous "Bear Flag Revolt." Two years later he joined the rush of 1848 to the Sierra foothills and came out with $25,000 in gold dust, enough to buy his Red Bluff Ranch and to build an adobe home on the banks of the Sacramento River near the present-day town of Red Bluff.

From farmer to revolutionary to argonaut to rancher, Ide then became a "Roy Bean"-style justice of the peace for Colusi County (now Colusa, Glenn, and Tehama counties). Being a dedicated man of public service in this sparsely populated country meant that Ide filled many positions at once. One account reads that "In a trial of a horse thief, he acted as judge, court, clerk, prosecutor, and defense attorney—he raised legal points for both sides, gave his rulings as judge, and then, as court clerk, recorded the proceedings. The jury found the defendant guilty, and Ide, as judge, sentenced him to hang." Unorthodox, yes, but that was the California frontier.

The William B. Ide Adobe has been restored to depict the life and times of its founder. Built from the surrounding earth, it aptly shows that even simple homes can be great monuments.

Bidwell Mansion State Historic Park

Here lived John and Annie Bidwell, always ahead of their time and fighting to make a better

Bidwell Mansion, right, the most venerated building in Chico, opens its doors to the visiting public with the same graciousness that its founders, John and Annie Bidwell, two of California's leading citizens, greeted their guests in the late 1800s. WILLARD CLAY

America. Their three-story, 26-room Victorian mansion stands in Chico, the city founded by John Bidwell. Teacher, pioneer, soldier, statesman, politician, and philanthropist, Bidwell enjoyed a life of adventure and prosperity only California could offer. Above everything else, though, he considered himself a farmer. The soil was his ultimate wellspring of contentment.

His massive Rancho Chico, with the mansion as its focal point, was a grand experiment in horticultural and technical diversity, forming what many people believed was the "most famous and highly diversified agricultural enterprise in California." Asa Gray, preeminent American botanist, came to visit, as did Sir Joseph Hooker from London's prestigious Kew Gardens. John Muir, the enlightened naturalist and founder of the Sierra Club, enjoyed his time with the Bidwells, and Susan B. Anthony, champion of women's suffrage, found in them a common desire for equality. When U.S. presidents needed confidants in California, they turned to John and Annie Bidwell.

In 1841, with the clothes on his back, $75, and "nothing more formidable than a pocket knife," John Bidwell led the first wagon train west to California. He was a handsome, 21-year-old school teacher with an instinct for leadership and integrity. Seven years later, on a sandy bar of the Feather River, he discovered one of the richest strikes of the California gold rush.

Never a frivolous man, he invested his fortune in Rancho Chico while at the same time his career in public service skyrocketed, taking him to Washington, D.C., as a lobbyist for California statehood and later as a U.S. congressman. Head and shoulders above corruption, Bidwell might have won his campaigns for governor of California and president of the United States had he conceded to play dirty politics like his competitors. Bamboozled and lampooned to the point where "nice guys finish last," he slipped back into his life as a farmer.

Daily tours during the summer lead visitors through the spacious rooms of Vikingsholm, left, on the shore of Lake Tahoe's Emerald Bay. Designed after an eleventh-century Norse fortress, it was built in 1929 by a crew of 200 workmen. KEN McKOWEN

The lake within the lake, Emerald Bay, right, is probably the single most photographed part of Lake Tahoe. Fannette Island has a teahouse where Lora Knight, the owner of Vikingsholm, would take her guests for an afternoon treat. JEFF GNASS

Rancho Chico was a masterpiece of agrarian prosperity. Sixty miles of wooden fence partitioned over 20,000 acres of fields planted in wheat, barley, oats, and grapes (used for raisins, not wine, since Bidwell was a prohibitionist). A hundred men tended the crops and the 1,500 cows, 2,000 hogs, 3,000 sheep, and 300 horses. It was more a village than a farm—with its huge flour mill, experimental nursery, and horse-drawn combines—and everybody who was anybody passing through the northern Sacramento Valley made certain to stop and see Rancho Chico and Bidwell Mansion.

That same attraction persists today. The farm is gone, but the mansion still stands with its romantic, Italian villa design. It became a school for the Presbyterian church for a while, and after that a girls dormitory for Chico State University. In 1964 the California State Park System acquired the mansion and, together with private organizations, has restored and refurbished it to 90 percent of its original flavor.

Vikingsholm (Emerald Bay State Park)

Lake Tahoe's Emerald Bay reminded her of a Norwegian fjord, so Mrs. Lora J. Knight decided to design her summer home appropriately.

Called "Tahoe's Hidden Castle," and "one of the finest examples of Scandinavian architecture existing in the United States," Vikingsholm stands like an eleventh-century Norse fortress among stately firs and pines. Built in the summer of 1929 by 200 skilled workers (many of them Scandinavians), it is as solid now as it was then. The great stone walls rise into steep, wood-shingled roofs. Spokes of sunlight spill through leaded windows. Inside, modern conveniences are married to medieval motifs. Carved dragon heads hang from the beams. Each room has hand-wrought light fixtures and door latches. A circular Chinese cashmere rug (that cost Mrs. Knight $40,000 in the thirties) graces the library. There is a three-legged peasant chair, a bridal table, a carved balustrade, and "Selma," the Finnish clock. When the governments of Norway and Sweden declined Mrs. Knight's requests for museum antiques for Vikingsholm, she had craftsmen make exact replicas.

Riding on a fortune made by her father in railroads and foods, Mrs. Knight spared no expense on her summer home. She employed a staff of 15 and consistently entertained six to ten guests. Mrs. Knight lived and shared her regal life

at Vikingsholm for 16 joyous summers until she died in 1945 at the age of 82.

Ehrman Mansion (Sugar Pine Point State Park)

Any man who is director of three banks, president of two more, and chairman of the board of yet another is bound to need a sumptuous retreat where he can get away from it all. Enter Isaias W. Hellman and his Pine Lodge.

From the heart of his financial empire in downtown San Francisco, Hellman quietly purchased 2,000 acres on Lake Tahoe's Sugar Pine Point and supervised *in absentia* the construction of what many people still believe is "Tahoe's finest summer home." Completed in 1903, Pine Lodge later became the Ehrman Mansion when Hellman's youngest child, Florence, married Sidney Ehrman, an energetic, effervescent lawyer from San Francisco.

Roughly 50 guests received invitations each summer to stay at the Ehrman Mansion. Reclining in leather-covered chairs on polished hardwood floors, enjoying cocktails on the porch or at the fireplace, playing the nonelectric pinball machine called Klondike, or just sitting on the shore with feet in the lake and back to the sun, guests no doubt found life at the Ehrman Mansion to be exactly what it was intended to be—sumptuous.

Later weakened by a stroke, Mrs. Ehrman nevertheless met with her staff every morning to plan the day's schedule.

She strolled along the trails to pick dandelions, which she disliked to no end, and used her $10,000 birdcage elevator in lieu of the stairs. Mr. Ehrman never did slow down. At 83 he was berated by his doctor for swimming out in the middle of the lake. And at 100 he shaved his beard, saying it made him look too old. He died at the age of 101 in 1975.

Vikingsholm and Ehrman Mansion are more than fine pieces of architecture. They are tributes to the people—Mrs. Knight, the Hellmans, and the

Ehrmans—who created something in harmony, not in competition, with Lake Tahoe.

Adamson House (Malibu Lagoon State Beach)

Take a blend of Spanish, Moorish, and Persian motifs, distill them into a home that is considered the crème de la crème of ceramic-tile architecture, and preserve it all on a breathtaking California beach. This is Adamson House, something Picasso might have created had he worked with tiles rather than brushes. Every fringe and hollow from floor to ceiling is a study in exquisite detail. The patterns, or arabesques, somehow interweave abstract geometries into simple harmonies highlighted by brilliant, living colors. In one corner of a bathroom alone there are seven different designs of Malibu tile, yet they fit together beautifully. And complimenting them are teakwood doors, bottle-glass windows, and filigree ironworks, each carved, framed, or wrought by hand. Tour leaders here are accustomed to visitors walking about with eyes wide open and mouths agape. Adamson House has a habit, after all, of exceeding expectations.

The word famous has powerful connotations. We imagine huge, opulent castles built without the least concern for cost. For the most part that's true. But for some, like William B. Ide, a simple adobe ranch house was sufficient.

William B. Bourn, Jr., on the other hand, called his magnificent, 15-room retreat at Empire Mine a "cottage." Most visitors choke when they hear that. Today, gentlemen in twenties' top hats and overcoats drive antique cars up to the Empire Cottage in unforgettable living history demonstrations.

Many of the Spanish-Mexican homes, like Lachryma Montis in Sonoma, where General Mariano Vallejo retired, and his Petaluma Adobe and Pio Pico's El Ranchito, were places of surrender where great lives ended in comparative poverty, not riches. At times a sense of melancholy pervades them.

Other homes can leave us with inescapable feelings of loss. They are places where brilliant men found the inspirations they shared with the world and where their lives ended too soon. What more might Jack London have given us had he lived his allotted years? And Will Rogers?

In joy and sorrow, wealth and poverty, society and solitude, the lives of famous Californians seem a heartbeat away in their homes. The vicarious experience is a little intoxicating. It's easy to open the imagination and go back 50 years; suddenly you are in the Baroque portal between the Main Vestibule and the Assembly Room, and William Randolph Hearst is offering you a glass of wine. ∎

Moss-covered rocks, left, line the banks of Burney Creek in McAuthur-Burney Falls Memorial State Park in northern California. JEFF GNASS

Working from a rocky point near Malibu, far left, these fishermen could be trying for barred surf perch, California cordina, opal eye, or calico bass. ED COOPER

The noblest of a noble race

"These trees are the botanical equivalent of dinosaurs," says Joseph H. Engbeck, Jr., who has written extensively on the California State Park System. "That's how long they've been around, a good hundred and sixty million years or so. They're not just marvels of size and beauty and individual age, but of evolutionary age as well."

Redwoods—looking much as they do today— have been on this planet 30 times longer than the Grand Canyon and 15,000 times longer than Yosemite Valley. Visitors walking into a grove of them enter a time warp. The cool, damp, dimly lit forest harkens back to the ancient Mesozoic period when redwoods first evolved. Green infuses everything in those groves, even the air. The silence hangs like the moss, grandfatherly and almost within human reach, as if put there by the light touch of a masterful hand.

"They evoke a kind of reverence accorded no other American tree," Elna Bakker writes in *An Island Called California*. "Their groves have been called temples and their spires cathedral-like; every writer describing them is lavish with vocabulary borrowed from church architecture."

But no words seem adequate; perhaps because our language evolved in a world without such trees. How can comparisons to a church be made when the trees not only outdate the church, but the religion as well? Ask the men who build cathedrals to build a redwood of average size, say 220 feet high and 15 feet thick at its base. Let it sway in the wind and scent the air. Let it drink and breathe from the sky and the soil. Let it age from the time of Christ, surrounded by thousands of others like it rising into the fog and rain. Rising out of sight. This is where the adjectives have failed. This is where the old feel young, the anxious feel calm, the indifferent feel respect.

"Save the Redwoods," came the cry of the turn-of-the-century conservationists who realized America was losing one of her greatest natural heritages. Trees growing for a thousand years were routinely felled in a day. Photographs of the loggers standing atop the fallen giants, their arms akimbo, their manners a bit macho, hit a raw nerve among those who regarded redwoods as something far more important than board feet of lumber. Redwoods have rights, they said, and it's time to let them be. "Any fool can destroy a tree," wrote John Muir. "They cannot defend themselves or run away. These kings of the forest, the noblest of a noble race, rightly belong to the world. As they are in California, we cannot escape the responsiblity as their guardians."

The responsibility began in 1864 when President Abraham Lincoln signed an act of Congress

A hygrophorus mushroom splashes scarlet onto the forest floor of Armstrong Redwoods State Reserve, just 90 minutes north of San Francisco in Sonoma County. This forest gained early protection when Colonel James Armstrong, a lumberman, set it aside in the 1870s as "a natural park and botanic garden." D. CAVAGNARO

creating Yosemite Valley and the adjacent Mariposa Big Tree Grove of giant sequoias as the nation's first state parks. (They were later given federal protection within Yosemite National Park.) Concerned citizens in northern California formed the Sempervirens Club (named after the scientific species name of the coast redwood) in 1900, and two years later their efforts bore fruit when the state legislature created California Redwood Park, a precursor of Big Basin Redwoods State Park. It preserved many redwoods approaching 300 feet in height.

Still, up and down the coast the giant trees fell like dominoes as the sounds of long crosscut saws echoed through the forest. In 1917 a different breed of men discovered the redwoods. They were distinguished American scientists and conservationists who traveled together and visited the magnificient redwood groves of Humboldt and Del Norte counties.

Inspired by the trees and infuriated by the logging, they awakened the nation to the beauty and the plight of the redwoods with a timely article in a 1918 issue of *National Geographic* magazine. That same year they organized the Save-the-Redwoods League, "with its objective," says current Executive Director John B. Dewitt, "to rescue from destruction representative areas of primeval forests and to cooperate with state and national park services in establishing redwood parks."

Little did anyone realize in 1918 that it would take 50 long years of political attrition before a coast redwoods national park was established. Yet

Braided like rope, the soft, fibrous, stringy bark of a coast redwood climbs into the sky. Insect and infection proof, up to a foot thick, and nearly as resistent to fire as asbestos, it protects the tree against all attackers, save man. The bark on this tree is more gray than red, denoting a tree of tremendous age, possibly over a thousand years.

ED COOPER

many important battles were won over those years as grove after grove of magnificent trees gained protection through the efforts of the Save-the-Redwoods League, the Garden Club of America, the State of California, and the National Geographic Society. These groves became the nuclei around which were formed many of California's redwood state parks.

The protection came none too early. In 1964 the U.S. Department of the Interior issued a report of sobering statistics: of California's 2,000,000 acres of *original* redwood forest, only 300,000 acres (one seventh) remained. Today, 50,000 of those acres are in 31 state parks.

Only one state park, Calaveras Big Trees, has the giant sequoia. The sequoia differs from its coastal cousin in several ways. It has a wider girth but is not as tall. It reproduces from seed only (about 200 to each cone; about 90,000 to a pound), whereas the coast redwood often reproduces by stump sprouting. The coast redwood also reproduces by seed: about 123,000 to a pound.

The sequoia is a mountain tree confined to 75 isolated groves between 4,500 and 8,000 feet on the west slope of the Sierra Nevada. The redwood "follows the fog" along the coast, preferring year-round moist weather. Both live to old age, but the sequoia more so. It can reach 3,000 years while the coast redwood might reach 2,000. Between the two—giant sequoia and coast redwood—California can boast having the world's largest and tallest living organisms.

Humboldt Redwoods State Park

The largest of California's redwood parks (51,000 acres), Humboldt is as much a testament to the people who save great trees as it is to the trees themselves. Of the approximately 600 memorial groves established with the help of the Save-the-Redwoods League, over 100 are in this park. The 9,000-acre Rockefeller Forest, for example, was purchased from the Pacific Lumber Company with a $1 million private donation and

matching funds from the 1928 California State Park Bond Act. Many of the trees rise over 300 feet, and the tallest, appropriately called the Tall Tree, crowns out at 359 feet. Several other groves—the Founders, the Garden Club of America, the Kent-Mather, and the Newton B. Drury—commemorate the men and women who pioneered a national appreciation for living redwood trees.

Probably the most famous feature in Humboldt Redwoods State Park is the 33-mile-long Avenue of the Giants (which, by the way, is a spectacular alternate route to Highway 101). The tall trees are broken here and there by quiet meadows and pull-off areas for picnicking and hiking, and through it all flows the peaceful Eel River.

Prairie Creek Redwoods State Park

"A second gold," miners called the redwoods in the 1850s. Having wandered out of the mother lode country after their boom turned to bust, these men were hungry for new riches. The coastal tall trees caught their eye. Attempts had been made

*The dreaded poison oak (*Rhus diversiloba*) can take on a remarkable phase when it turns scarlet and climbs the trunks of redwoods, left, up to 150 feet high. Tolerant of both sun and shade and distinguished by its three-parted, glossy leaves, poison oak ranges up and down California's coast and can readily ruin a walk through the woods.*
LARRY ULRICH

Golden bluffs greet the sea along the coast at Prairie Creek Redwoods State Park, right, about five miles north of Orick. Accessible via the Davidson Road through the southern end of the park, Gold Bluffs Beach is a favorite hideout of coast connoisseurs. Campsites are available, and nearby is the entrance to Fern Canyon, which cuts through the bluffs to form 50-foot-high walls draped in mosses and ferns and carpeted in horsetails. KAZ HAGIWARA

A herd of Roosevelt elk, top, grazes near Gold Bluffs Beach at Prairie Creek Redwoods State Park. Named in honor of President Theodore Roosevelt, they were threatened with extinction until conservation efforts saved them in the early 1900s. LARRY ULRICH

Sailboard enthusiasts ride the waves and the wind off Waddell Beach, bottom, at Big Basin Redwoods State Park, about 20 miles north of Santa Cruz. GEORGE WUERTHNER

earlier by the Russians and Spanish to cut and mill the trees, but their successes had been limited. Leave it to the '49ers—Americans of French, Scottish, British, and Scandinavian stock—to employ their ingenuity and improved tools to attack the trees. At first it took a two-man team a week of 10-hour days to fall a redwood. But cutting methods quickly improved. The handsome lumber was in big demand (for fledgling towns like San Francisco), and there was no time to waste. The redwood lumber industry was born overnight.

It's a miracle that the redwoods in such places as Prairie Creek, 50 miles north of Eureka, survived. The Save-the-Redwoods League purchased the first groves here in 1923, and with the cooperation of the California State Park Commission, a second purchase was made in 1932. The park today is a hallmark of natural history interpretation with its self-guided Revelation Trail for the blind, complete with "please-touch-me" features described both on signs and in braille.

Seventy miles of trails wander through a dozen memorial and honor groves. And on the park's seaward side a dirt road descends to Gold Bluffs Beach from which visitors can reach Fern Canyon, a grotto of fern-draped walls 50 feet high.

Watch for Roosevelt elk, the largest land animal in California. Named for President Theodore Roosevelt, the elk came face to face with extinction 80 years ago when white settlers decimated them for meat and hides. The elks' teeth were in demand as good luck charms, and the 40-pound multi-pointed antlers of the bulls attracted trophy hunters from around the country. Things are different now. State law prohibits even approaching the elk.

Big Basin Redwoods State Park

In October 1769 the sickly, half-starved expedition of Gaspar de Portolá arrived at the mouth of Waddell Creek on the Pacific Coast, 20 miles north of present-day Santa Cruz. They were the first Spaniards to enter California and explore its coast by foot. For several days they camped beneath what Portolá declared were "the thickest, tallest, straightest trees they had ever seen." By the time they left, headed north to discover San Francisco Bay, their illnesses were gone. They named the place "Cañada de la Salud"—Canyon of Health.

Waddell Creek today delineates a portion of the southern boundary of 16,000-acre Big Basin Redwoods State Park. Created in 1902, it's the oldest park in the state system. Denzil Verardo, a state park ranger, wrote in 1985, "It was here, in Big Basin, that the initial successful effort to save coast redwoods occurred. It was here that the dynamic fight to purchase a park took place, and it was here that Californians finally saw their unmatchable coast redwoods, their heritage, protected for all time."

The battle isn't over; it never is. Inholdings in Big Basin have escaped development several times (thanks to the Sempervirens Fund), but other private inholdings still exist. The state hopes to acquire them to create someday a fully protected watershed within the park.

Like every other redwood park, Big Basin has a lot more than tall trees. Plant communities range from marshland to riparian (streamside) to chaparral to redwood. One hundred miles of trails thread through it all. There are about a dozen

"These great trees belong to the silences and the millenniums," wrote Edwin Markham in **California the Wonderful.** *"Many of them have seen more than a hundred of our generations rise, and give out their little clamors and perish. They chide our pettiness, they rebuke our impiety. They seem, indeed, to be forms of immortality standing here among the transitory shapes of time." Here along the North Escape Road, right, they stand like sentinels in Big Basin Redwoods State Park.* LARRY ULRICH

species of amphibians and reptiles (most of them shy) and a dozen species of mammals (most of them shy, as well).

The birds, however, seldom go unnoticed. If their colors don't get attention, their calls and songs will. It was in Big Basin, in fact, that the first nest of a marbled murrelet was discovered. A small, demure, nondescript seabird (related to puffins and murres), the murrelet had baffled ornithologists for decades. The nests of every other North American breeding bird had been found, except that of a marbled murrelet. No one expected it to be in evergreen trees. The recent discovery in Big Basin was a landmark event. It delighted the world of birdwatchers (who had begun to wonder if the murrelets reproduced by replication, like algae) and made big headlines in every American ornithological forum.

Calaveras Big Trees State Park

The story goes that A.T. Dowd, hunter, adventurer, and raconteur, was chasing a wounded bear when he stumbled into a grove of trees "bigger than an ordinary man can imagine" in the Sierra Nevada foothills of Calaveras County. Dowd stopped dead in his tracks and stood there, stunned. He had discovered the other redwood— the giant sequoia.

Here was a newspaper story reporters from back East wouldn't have to exaggerate, but they did anyway. The trees truly were 300 feet high, 25 feet in basal diameter, and 2,000 to 3,000 years old. People thought it was a hoax.

What better way, then, to prove to America the size of the giant sequoias than to cut one down and section out a piece of the trunk for a traveling exhibit? In 1853 a group of men with dollar signs in their eyes did just that. It took five of them 23 days with augers, saws, and axes to fall A.T. Dowd's "Discovery Tree." It was the first giant sequoia ever felled by white men.

Local folks later used the 24-foot stump as a dance floor while A.T. Dowd and a few others, including the young conservationist, John Muir, shook their heads in disgust. The sectioned trunk was exhibited in San Francisco and New York City, but the whole affair turned into a financial and environmental disaster.

But that didn't dissuade a second group the next year. They girdled 116 vertical feet of thick bark from the "Mother-of-the-Forest" tree (one of the largest and most symmetrical sequoias in the North Grove of the park today) and reassembled it to impress the gentry in San Francisco and New York. The popular exhibit was shipped to London in 1857 and received by enthusiastic audiences in the prestigious Crystal Palace. British imperialism being what it was, even among the ranks of its scientists, prompted English botanists to insist the great tree be named Wellingtonia, in honor of their hero who had defeated Napoleon at Waterloo. But the rules of botanical nomenclature prevailed, and the giant sequoia received the scientific name it retains today, *Sequoiadendron giganteum*. Meanwhile, the Mother-of-the-Forest tree, stripped of her protective and life-giving bark, had died.

At a meeting of the American Association for the Advancement of Science in New York in 1876, John Muir delivered a scientific paper that ended with a caveat: that although the giant sequoia, "the Forest King, had survived the Ice Age and might live gloriously on in Nature's keeping, it is rapidly vanishing before the fire and steel of man; and unless protective measures be speedily invented and applied, in a few decades at the farthest, all that will be left of the sequoia will be a few hacked and scarred monuments." There was no doubt in anyone's mind that Muir was speaking about the Calaveras Groves. It was time for the world to awaken from what he called a "death-like apathy."

The Calaveras were the first discovered and hence the best-known groves of giant sequoia. Public sentiment grew fast, thanks to spokesmen like Muir, and at the slightest whisper of

The first state park

In June 1864, while America was spilling her blood in the Civil War, an obscure but history-making bill moved without opposition through Congress and arrived at the desk of President Abraham Lincoln. The bill was a land grant from the federal government to the young State of California to preserve, not develop, 20,000 acres around the "Yosemite Gorge" and the adjacent Mariposa Grove of giant sequoias— Yosemite State Park.

Authored by California Senator John Conness, the grant was made "under the express conditions that the premises shall be held for public use, resort, and recreation, and shall be inalienable for all time." Historian and author Joseph H. Engbeck, Jr., writes, "thus, quietly and without controversy, in the shadow of a dark moment of our history, the nation's first state park was created. . . ."

Over the years, public sentiment grew in favor of federal control of Yosemite. John Muir, founder of the Sierra Club and an undying advocate of the strict preservation of Yosemite, believed the park should "be taken wholly out of the governor's hands. The office changes too often and must always be more or less mixed with politics in its bearing upon appointments for the valley." Among his eager listeners was President Theodore Roosevelt, who visited the park in 1903. Three years later, Roosevelt signed legislation that integrated Yosemite Valley and the Mariposa Grove of Big Trees into a national park.

California's stewardship in Yosemite was over, but the seed of commitment to preserving its natural, historical, and scenic wonders had taken root. Over the decades it would grow into a sterling collection of state parks hardly imaginable in John Muir's time.

Visitors literally stroll through a giant sequoia in the famous North Grove of Calaveras Big Trees State Park, the only unit in the California State Park System that preserves giant sequoias. Interpretive trails here in the summer become popular cross-country skiing routes in the winter.
KEN McKOWEN

auctioning the trees to lumbermen, a majority of Californians protested. It took decades of tireless effort to finally see the ceremonial dedication of Calaveras Big Trees State Park in July 1931. The prized South Grove was absorbed into the park in August 1954. The transaction cost $28 million.

William Penn Mott, Jr., former director of the California State Park System, wrote in 1973, "Half a dozen presidents of the United States and several governors have had a hand in trying to save the Calaveras Groves. Many legislators on the state and federal level have worked on the problems as have thousands of citizens. Today, after years of effort, it can be said—cautiously—that the Calaveras Big Trees have been saved."

The 5,900-acre park contains two groves of giant sequoias: the famous North Grove with the Mother-of-the-Forest tree and Big Stump (formerly A.T. Dowd's Discovery Tree), and the larger yet less visited South Grove, which was designated as a natural preserve in 1984, the highest level of land protection in the California State Park System.

Pine forests, lava bluffs, several creeks and streams, and the Stanislaus River add further dimensions to the park. Each season has its highlights. Dogwood and azalea blossom in spring. Woodpeckers, chickadees, squirrels, and chipmunks chatter in summer. Delicate colors hint at autumn, and a soft blanket of snow falls in winter, tracked here and there where rangers have led visitors on snowshoes and cross-country skis through groves of trees "bigger than an ordinary man can imagine."

The redwoods were the catalyst that started the California State Park System. It was a mandate of the people who wanted a heritage saved. Protected groves became parks, and the parks grew into a system without equal. From Jedediah Smith and Del Norte Coast redwoods, near Crescent City in the north, to Pfeiffer Big Sur and Julia Pfeiffer Burns in the south, a chain of 31 parks protects valuable pockets of redwoods along California's coast.

Surrounding the San Francisco Bay Area are Armstrong Redwoods, Samuel P. Taylor, and Mount Tamalpais state parks to the north, and to the south are Portola, Butano, Big Basin Redwoods, and Henry Cowell Redwoods state parks.

There are more to these parks than tall trees. A redwood forest isn't marvelous just in height. The understory has its charm, too. Beneath the kingly green canopy grow colorful splashes of rhododendrons, dogwoods, trilliums, azaleas, lilacs, and orchids. Nor is a redwood forest a zoological desert. Many species of mammals and birds frequent the groves, and others pass through during spring and fall migrations. These places aren't museums or artificial gardens; they're living systems of wild plants and animals crowned high in the sky by the coast redwood and the giant sequoia. ∎

Two types of trees

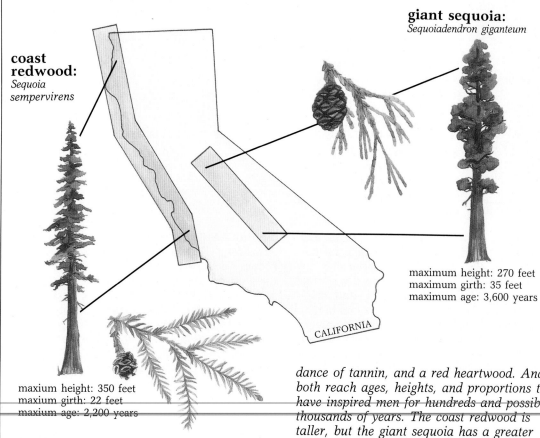

coast redwood:
Sequoia sempervirens

giant sequoia:
Sequoiadendron giganteum

CALIFORNIA

maximum height: 270 feet
maximum girth: 35 feet
maximum age: 3,600 years

maxium height: 350 feet
maxium girth: 22 feet
maxium age: 2,200 years

The rhododendron blooming in Kruse Rhododendron State Park is thriving due to an early burn which destroyed much of the forest. The second-growth of redwood, Douglas fir, and tan oak is now threatening to choke out the rhododendron and jeopardize the annual floral display.
FRANK S. BALTHIS

Call them cousins—the redwoods of the California Coast and the giant sequoia of the western Sierra Nevada foothills. Both are cone-bearing evergreens with a reddish, fibrous bark, a lack of resin cells, an abundance of tannin, and a red heartwood. And both reach ages, heights, and proportions that have inspired men for hundreds and possibly thousands of years. The coast redwood is taller, but the giant sequoia has a greater wood volume and attains an older age.

They occupy different habitats—the redwood preferring the moist maritime climate of the coast, and the giant sequoia growing in 75 separate groves between 4,500 and 8,000 feet in the Sierra Nevada.

The delicate sword fern, above, (Polystichum munitum) is a common forest floor resident of California's redwood state parks. JEFF FOOTT

Sunlight filters through the morning mist to gently stir campers at Patrick's Point State Park. A day of hiking on any of the park's 12 trails awaits these late risers. Azalea, rhododendron, salal, and thick patches of blackberry and huckleberry are just part of the abundant flora that make up the lush, almost impenetrable habitat at Patrick's Point State Park. FRANK S. BALTHIS

The incomparable coast

Nothing is more distinctly Californian than her coast. The steep, fog-swept cliffs in the north break into a long refrain of sunstruck beaches in the south. Along the 1,264 miles are countless inventions of seashore—from tidepools and sea stacks to marshes and mudflats. It's salty, high-spirited country that brings out wild oats in some and moods of pensive contemplation in others.

The state park system has more than 100 coastal units comprising roughly one sixth of California's ocean shore. The names of the more famous read like a list of "Great American Seascapes"—Big Sur, Point Lobos, Morro Bay, San Simeon, Salt Point,

Patrick's Point, and Año Nuevo. There are 70 state beaches, 60 of them south of San Francisco. But not all the units hug the coast. Many lie hidden slightly inland and protect valuable pieces of habitat. Foremost among them are Azalea, Kruse Rhododendron, Jug Handle (with its "ecological staircase"), and Los Osos Oaks state reserves and Andrew Molera, Sinkyone Wilderness, and Van Damme state parks.

Point Lobos State Reserve

Point Lobos, three miles south of Carmel, brings out the painter, the poet, and the philosopher in us. Francis McComas, the landscape artist, calls it "the greatest meeting of land and water in the world." Robinson Jeffers writes, "it flows out of mystery into mystery: there is no beginning—How could there be? And no end—how could there be?" Frederick Law Olmsted, Jr., remembered, "When the seas are running high, as they often do at Point Lobos, the huge waves, with their heaving, burst, and drag, grip the attention and rouse the emotions." Even the master storyteller Robert Louis Stevenson is rumored to have based his descriptions of *Treasure Island* on the forests and rocky ramparts of Point Lobos.

Punta de Lobos Marinos—Point of the Sea Wolves—derives its name from the barking calls of sea lions that carry inland on salted air from the offshore rocks. Out there with them are harbor seals and the once nearly extinct sea otter. Point Lobos is in fact one of the best places (along with Big Sur) on the coast of California to see sea otters. They frolic in the kelp beds and at the edge of the surf, floating belly side up while using a rock as an anvil to crack open their preferred foods: mussels, snails, crabs, chitons, abalones, and sea urchins. The thick rich fur that enables them to survive in waters from California to Alaska also brought a handsome price and led to their near demise at the hands of eighteenth- and nineteenth-century Russian, Yankee, and British fur traders. Tens of thousands were killed. Their recovery has been slow but the prognosis looks promising.

Point Lobos is as rich on land as it is at sea, with a species count of 22 terrestrial mammals, 3 salamanders, 2 toads, 2 lizards, and 3 snakes. Over 150 species of birds have been recorded. Hardly another piece of shoreline of equal size could be

Wild iris, one of California's more flamboyant wildflowers, grows in moist soils throughout the state. D. CAVAGNARO

Herring gulls, black oystercatchers, and willets, above, make a living on the rocky shore at Salt Point State Park, near Fort Ross, about 100 miles north of the Golden Gate. LARRY ULRICH

Ribs of sedimentary rock challenge the sea at Montaña de Oro State Park, right, at the southern end of Morro Bay. Several trails wind inland and along, the shore of this 10,000-acre park, some climbing up Alan, Oats, and Valencia peaks where 100 miles of coastline come into view. CARR CLIFTON

a more exciting distillation of diverse life forms. The habitats blend from island and shore into grassland, brushland, and forest. California poppies go mad here, erupting in the spring among brilliant splashes of goldfields, Indian paintbrush, and other wildflowers.

The most venerated member of the Point Lobos community is the Monterey cypress, a rare native tree carved into improbable shapes by the winds and salts. The weathered, talon-like branches reach into the leeward sky just as fingers of the rocky headlands reach into the sea. The cypress reminds us that mere survival is a hard battle here. The signatures of attrition are everywhere—in the wood, in the rocks, and in the rutted trails and the trampled vegetation.

"The timeless battering and grinding of the sea upon the shore is one of the most powerful, persistent and dramatic of the natural processes characteristic of Point Lobos," wrote Frederick Law Olmsted, Jr., *a nationally acclaimed landscape architect who directed the offical 1927-29 California State Park Survey. Although it is small, Point Lobos excells at diversity and can absorb entire afternoons of visitors who arrive intending to stay for only an hour or so.* GEORGE WUERTHNER

spectacular cliffs, wonderful waterfalls, magical fog, breathtaking vistas, dizzying heights, and quaint lifestyles. It's all accurate.

Maybe that's why we go to Big Sur and why we never forget it once we've been there. It brings out the child in us. And at the heart of all those adjectives are two state parks: Pfeiffer Big Sur and Julia Pfeiffer Burns.

Michael Pfeiffer wanted to be a cattle rancher. He left Marin County in 1869 and moved to the wild south coast of Big Sur, a four-day trip on a rough trail from Monterey. The fewer people the better, he thought, and he built his home at the mouth of Sycamore Canyon. At his side was his son, John, and his daughter, Julia, whose courage, intelligence, and gentle disposition would be forged over many years of hard work and good living. Like other families moving into the Big Sur country—the McWays, Burns, Andersons, Posts, and Partingtons—the Pfeiffers supported themselves by farming, ranching, beekeeping, and lumbering. Their ways have hardly changed.

"For the first time in my life," Robinson Jeffers writes about Big Sur in *Not Man Apart*, "I could see people living—amid magnificent, unspoiled scenery—essentially as they did in the Idylls and the Sagas, or in Homer's Ithaca. Here was life purged of the ephemeral accretions. Men were riding after cattle, or plowing the headland, hovered by white sea-gulls, as they have done for thousands of years, and will do for thousands of years to come. Here was contemporary life that was also permanent life, and not shut off from the modern world but conscious of it and related to it, capable of expressing its spirit—but unencumbered by the mass of poetically irrelevant details

Like Yosemite Valley, Point Lobos is an extremely popular place that gets more visitors than are good for it. The solution, though, is not to kick all the people out, but to carefully manage their numbers over critical periods of time. There is a lot of philosophical space at Point Lobos— temporal and physical worlds that inspire, touch, and change us.

It reminds us that America is and must remain more than a nation of people, cats, and dogs.

There is a balance to be found between providing and protecting places like Point Lobos.

The California Department of Parks and Recreation is determined to maintain that balance. Then, and only then, will our descendants discover in the weathered cypress and the frolicking sea otter the inspirations we find today.

Pfeiffer Big Sur and Julia Pfeiffer Burns State Parks

Writers learn early not to be excessive with adjectives. It's verbs that make good prose, they are told, not adjectives. But the lessons crumble when they visit Big Sur and wax poetic about

A profile of pinnipeds

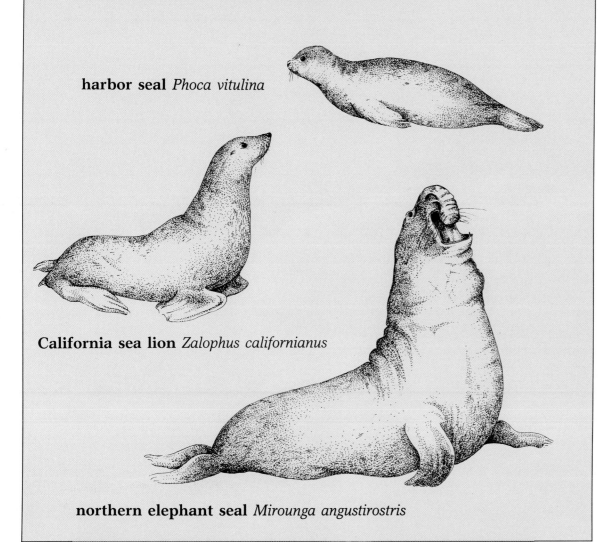

harbor seal *Phoca vitulina*

California sea lion *Zalophus californianus*

northern elephant seal *Mirounga angustirostris*

The California coast is home to five species of pinnipeds—the California sea lion, Steller sea lion, northern fur seal, northern elephant seal, and harbor seal. Descendants of terrestrial carnivores that entered the sea in search of food 20 to 30 million years ago, they live a life of compromise today, feeding and swimming at sea, but resting and breeding on land, preferably on islands that afford protection from terrestrial predators.

The two species of sea lions are not difficult to tell apart if observed at the same place at the same time. The Steller is larger and less common. It ranges from Alaska to California, with Año Nuevo as its southernmost summer breeding site. California sea lions are two to three times smaller. They bark frequently while lounging on jetties, piers, spits, and islands. They range from the Farallon Islands south along Baja California to the west coast of Mexico. Subspecific populations, adapted to local conditions, are in Japan and the Galapagos Islands.

Northern elephant seals make a spectacle of themselves every winter when they come ashore to breed at Año Nuevo, the Farallon Islands, the Channel Islands, and points south along the coast of Mexico. The largest bulls weigh 5,000 pounds and measure up to 18 feet long.

At the opposite end of the scale is the harbor seal—small, shy, and wary. Often mistaken for yearling northern elephant seals, they inhabit bays and estuaries and other isolated pockets along the coast and seldom tolerate the close approach of humans.

Northern fur seals visit the California Coast in small numbers each winter. In Mexico they are called **lobos de dos pelos**—the wolves of two hairs, for the contrasting inner and outer layers of fur that insulate them in the cold Alaskan waters where they spend their summers.

and complexities that make a civilization."

The Esselen Indians had frequented this country for centuries, but apparently not in great numbers. The Spanish had avoided it altogether, calling it "El Pais Grande del Sur"—The Big Country of the South. But as the area's accessibility increased— the trail becoming a wagon road—so did its population and popularity. The two Pfeiffer children, John and Julia, went about their lives on the ragged edge of North America. Each married, built homes, and accrued the lands that eventually became the nuclei of the parks named after them.

Travelers tend to stroll through these parks, not walk. There's a lot to explore. Our senses open up, and we readily understand why the guidebooks say Big Sur is as much a feeling as it is a place. Trails pass through groves of redwoods and chaparral up to overlooks and down to the sea and along famous McWay Creek and Big Sur Gorge. The parks are small, but size makes no difference here. It's the intimacy that counts. Water ouzels (also called dippers—John Muir's favorite bird) and belted kingfishers feed in the creeks while somewhere overhead are crows, owls, hawks, and vultures.

Touted as the most scenic stretch of coastline in California, Big Sur, left, gains rugged definition beneath a brooding sky. Robinson Jeffers, Henry Miller, Jack Kerouac, and other iconoclastic writers found a sanctum sanctorum in these lonely, majestic sea bluffs—places that, with their help, retain to this day reputations of myth and reality. ED COOPER

From a popular scenic overlook at Julia Pfeiffer Burns State Park, a waterfall spills off Saddle Rock into McWay Cove, right. Cormorants, gulls, pelicans, oystercatchers, and guillemots are commonly seen here, but the biggest attraction (literally) might be the California gray whales that migrate south to warmer waters off Baja California in December and January.
LARRY ULRICH

The California gray whale (Eschrichtius gibbosus) migrates annually along the California Coast to its summer feeding grounds in the Bering Sea and its winter breeding grounds off Baja California. Several coastal state parks, from Patrick's Point up north to Torrey Pines down south, have become popular whale-watching sites as the leviathans pass within a mile or two of the shore. Biologists estimate the world population to be somewhere between 10,000 and 13,000. FRANK S. BALTHIS

The mammal life is equally rich: black-tailed deer, raccoons, gray squirrels, gray fox, and bobcats live in the forest. Grizzlies once roamed the Santa Lucia Mountains. Their absence lessens the wilderness integrity of Big Sur, and adding insult to injury, feral pigs have been introduced. They root up and destroy native vegetation, cause destructive erosion, eat the eggs and chicks of ground-nesting birds, and in general they disrupt the ecology and make a mess.

Still, the Big Sur parks are a paradise nonpareil with their nature trails, fitness trails, waterfall trails, homestead cabins, picnic areas, and environmental campsites.

The forest breathes in quiet counterpoint to the sea cliffs and pounding surf where Julia Pfeiffer Burns changes from a terrestrial park into an underwater marine preserve, abutted against the California Sea Otter State Game Refuge. Anxieties wash away here—gone in the fog, the rain, the sun, and the sea spray. After a short visit we realize that

although Big Sur has a big reputation, it has no trouble living up to it.

"It's the face of the earth as the creator intended it to look," long-time resident Henry Miller calls Big Sur. Once you've been there, you'll agree.

Año Nuevo State Reserve

"And how far is it to Point Año Nuevo?" a nineteenth-century traveler asked an old Indian near Pescadero.

"Oh, señor, it must be a very long way! I think it is in the neighborhood of the other world."

Things haven't changed. Located 27 miles south of Half Moon Bay, Año Nuevo is more accessible now than it was then, but it still belongs to another world. Where else can you pull off a scenic coast drive, take a short walk, and in a few minutes be standing among thousands of elephant seals? These likable animals with their dark, soulful eyes and long, bulbous snouts, looking like characters from the mind of Dr. Seuss, arrive every winter

at Año Nuevo to bring forth their new generation. It's one of the greatest wildlife spectacles in North America.

The history, geology, plant life, and intertidal zones of Año Nuevo are fascinating, too, as are the harbor seals and sea lions. But the 60,000 people that visit here from December to April don't come to see wildflowers and starfish; they come to see *Mirounga angustirostris*, the northern elephant seal, a species back from the brink of extinction. Californians, almost zany over these animals, have welcomed them back home with open arms.

That the seals are here at all is a miracle. Forty years ago not a single one could be found along the entire coast of California. The United States in the early 1800s was hungry for oil to lubricate the gears of her industrial revolution, and although whaling provided some, it wasn't enough. Enter the northern elephant seal, described as "large, slow, unafraid of humans and predictable in habit." Easy prey. One large bull rendered up to 210 gallons of oil, second in quality only to that of sperm whales.

Thus began the systematic slaughter called "elephanting," which continued every winter for almost half a century. By 1860 the elephant seal had been shot and clubbed to the point of economic exhaustion, and by 1869 none could be found anywhere in North America. Presumed forever gone, *M. angustirostris* was officially listed as "extinct" in 1884.

Imagine their surprise, then, when eight years later a Smithsonian scientific expedition discovered eight northern elephant seals on a remote beach on Mexico's Guadalupe Island, 150 miles southwest of the Baja peninsula. The scientists immediately shot seven, reasoning that the animals were "doomed to extinction...and few, if any, were to be found in the museums of North America." But somehow, somewhere, a few more elephant seals lay hidden on Guadalupe Island. To protect the seals the Mexican government posted soldiers there with orders to shoot first and ask questions later. The seals began to multiply, and they haven't stopped since.

It was a joyous day in July 1955 when Melvin Johansen of the Snow Museum in Oakland sighted four elephant seals on Año Nuevo Island. The number of seals at Año Nuevo has since increased at a logarithmic rate. Two pups were born on the island in 1961, 300 in 1970, and 1,200 in 1980. Overcrowding finally created a "No Vacancy" situation on the island, and the seals began to breed on the Año Nuevo mainland.

Journalists looking at this historic record have eagerly claimed that the northern elephant seal has "rocketed to the realm of numerical safety." But biologists remain skeptical. They see over 100,000 seals descended from probably fewer than 100. That's a lot of inbreeding. By passing through a "genetic bottleneck" the seals may have lost some ability to cope with diseases and changing, unstable environments.

Ongoing research of the Año Nuevo seal population will hopefully predict and prevent any future catastrophes.

The seals come ashore to molt, mate, and give birth. A pregnant cow gives birth to a single pup between mid-January and mid-February. The newborn pup weighs 60 to 90 pounds, is unable to swim, and begins to nurse immediately on a mother's milk that is 55 percent fat. Its weight doubles in 11 days; quadruples in 22. The mother, in turn, fasts for a month while nursing, and by the time she returns to the sea, she's lost 40 percent of her body weight.

Life isn't easy for a newborn pup. It might become separated from its mother, be attacked and rejected by other females, and left to starve. It might be crushed by fighting bulls that weigh 75 to 100 times more. Or it might be washed out to sea and drowned. Pup mortality at Año Nuevo is about 15 percent, but in 1983 when winter storms battered the coast, about 60 percent of the

*With a face only a mother could love, a subadult northern elephant seal (***Mirounga angustirostris***) basks in the sun at Año Nuevo State Reserve. Probably the single most popular wildlife attraction on the coast of California, tens of thousands of elephant seals arrive on the beach every winter at Año Nuevo, just north of Santa Cruz, to give birth and mate.* FRANS LANTING

Clammers bend their backs and test their skill on the beach near Año Nuevo State Reserve. FRANK S. BALTHIS

newborns died. The pups eventually learn to swim, of course. They leave the beaches long after the cows and bulls, usually in April or May.

When two full-grown bull elephant seals meet on a beach to do combat, the genetic future of their species is at stake. Each bull wants to mate with as many cows as possible. There's no monogamy here; instead, a dominance hierarchy has evolved wherein a champion bull gains a harem of 40 to 50 cows (the maximum number he can control and defend), while the loser usually gets nothing. Most elephant seal bulls never mate and produce offspring; they lick their wounds and retreat to quiet beaches. They may return to fight next week or next year or they may never return again, having died at sea from old age or from attack by orca or great white sharks.

At Año Nuevo the California Department of Parks and Recreation has established a commendable mangement system that affords maximum visitation with minimum impact. Volunteer guides (docents), trained in natural history and resource management, lead groups of people at specific intervals along well-groomed trails through the seal rookery. The total trip takes a couple hours. The scenery is superb. The stories are entertaining. And the wildlife is fantastic. Other places have

their seals, but no others are so approachable, so well protected, and so well interpreted as the elephants on the beach at Año Nuevo.

Torrey Pines State Reserve and State Beach

This is the last stand for the Torrey pine. Backed to the sea by 10,000 years of a warming climate and by 200 years of encroaching human civilization, it has nowhere else to go. *Pinus torreyana* is the world's rarest species of pine. Only about 6,000 survive in the wild, half of them here at Torrey Pines State Reserve, near Del Mar, the other half on Santa Rosa Island, 175 miles to the north.

Along the coast the trees are stunted and bent into shapes reminiscent of the Japanese art of bonsai. Inland, the more sheltered trees grow taller and straighter. "Seedling establishment is precarious," writes Elna Bakker in *An Island Called California.* "Much of the seed crop is consumed by California ground squirrels and other rodents, and 90 percent of the seedlings that attempt establishment fail to survive through the first year. Some die from summer drought, others from fungal infestation if there is too much moisture."

Fire is a friend to the Torrey pine. It reduces squirrel populations and competing tree species

while increasing soil nutrients and seed dispersal. Like many species of pine, the Torrey is semi-serotinous, a condition whereby a fire's heat influences the tightly closed cones to open and scatter seeds.

Two natural preserves exist within the reserve. One includes the finest groves of Torrey pines and has two excellent trails. The other protects pockets of the last remaining salt marshes and waterfowl habitats in southern California. Some of the birds that stop here are almost as rare as the weathered pines that surround them.

One visitor remarked that "when walking on the beach or admiring the pines or watching the birds, you hear the traffic zipping along Interstate 5 only a mile away, and you realize there's more to life than increasing its speed."

So what about the other 90-odd coastal park units? The beaches at Morro Bay, Monterey, and Malibu are some of the best in North America. Monterey Bay alone has 16 coastal parks, Morro Bay has 6, the coast around San Diego has at least 10, and from Los Angeles to Santa Barbara there are about 20.

A penumbra of lesser known parks fades up the coast to the rocky north. Things are less predictable up here, adding that special touch of intrigue that converts tourists into travelers. Take Patrick's Point, for example, 25 miles north of Eureka, with its seven sea stacks (isolated pinnacles of rock surrounded by water), colorful agates, forests and meadows, and its tentacled roots of Sitka spruce. It has all the beauty but none of the fame of Point Lobos.

And there are others. The Sonoma and Mendocino coasts are rich with breathe-easy respite. Russian Gulch and Van Damme state parks briefly touch the coast before climbing inland to protect such habitats as Fern Canyon, the Pygmy Forest, and the Cabbage Patch. And if the thin crowds still seem too thick, go to Sinkyone Wilderness State

Left, ice plant, grasses, and Torrey pines make a stand against the sun and sea spray on the sandstone cliffs of Torrey Pines State Reserve, 15 miles north of San Diego. GEORGE WUERTHNER

Killed by an oil spill, a common murre, above, lies in the hand of a park aid. FRANK S. BALTHIS

Park where visitors can "hike in only."

Such is the greatness of the California Coast. It adds up to a lot of fun and discovery. Many Californians—young and old—spend some of their finest days in the sand and surf or in the forests and meadows of their state beaches and parks. ■

A solitary fisherman casts into the surf at Sunset State Beach, top left. ALEXANDER LOWRY

Visitors at sunset, Santa Cruz Lighthouse Point, top right.
FRANK S. BALTHIS

Seventy state beaches offer their visitors the chance to make castles of their own, bottom left. WILLIAM HELSEL

Visitor at Año Nuevo poises with her camera, ready for whatever may happen next, bottom middle. FRANK S. BALTHIS

And it's another perfect day at Huntington Beach, bottom right. People-watching is the time-honored sport most practiced here.
CALIFORNIA DEPARTMENT OF PARKS AND RECREATION

More than a beacon to save lives, Pigeon Point Lighthouse, top, north of Santa Cruz near Año Nuevo State Reserve, moonlights as a hostel for travelers along the San Mateo Coast who wish to fall asleep to the sounds of the surf and sea lions. It's a popular place to stay for elephant seal enthusiasts planning to visit Año Nuevo the next morning, or for those who just wish to relax with idle walks up and down the beach. ED COOPER

The sea otter (Enhydra lutris), bottom, (a member of the weasel family) is slowly returning to the California Coast after a close call with extinction at the hands of fur traders 100 years ago. They have the endearing habit of floating on their backs while cracking open clams and other foods on their chests. JEFF FOOTT

Blue jewels

California wears her lakes like blue jewels. Look on a map to see how they ring the mountain ranges and sparkle the valleys, balanced from north to south and east to west in a nearly even distribution. The state park system has two dozen units covering 500 miles of lake frontage and 100 miles of river frontage. A park or recreation area might encompass an entire lake or, in most cases, only a small percentage of the shore or selected natural features. Some of the lakes, Mono and Tahoe especially, have serious health problems and need immediate public support. Others, most of them pooled behind dams, offer some of the best fishing and boating in California.

Mono Lake Tufa State Reserve

"Solemn, silent, sailless...the lonely tenant of the loneliest spot on Earth," wrote Mark Twain of Mono Lake in the 1860s. Californian Peter Steinhart, an essayist for *Audubon* magazine, calls Mono "a vast inland sea, a yawning, sage-covered afterthought of the snows that pile high atop the Sierra crest, seven miles to the west....Mono is the largest natural lake wholly within California. But in all this space, it seems small."

Mono is a lake of superlatives. Born of fire and ice and rimmed by a desert shore, it lies in the quiet embrace of a treeless, igneous land. Perhaps the oldest lake in North America, it has collected fresh creek water off the shoulders of the Sierra for at least 700,000 years. But the lake gives the water nowhere to go; there are no outlets. The water warms and evaporates into the high, dry desert sky, leaving behind salts and alkali. It's three times saltier than standard seawater and 50 times more alkaline. Swimmers float like wood on the surface. The early settlers called it a useless, pointless, fishless, lifeless place. "The Dead Sea of California."

*Red Fox (*Vulpes fulva*), left, prefers country with rolling hills, irregular meadows and semi-open woodland. It patrols this terrain for small rodents, ground-nesting birds, and fleshy fruit when in season.* D. CAVAGNARO

"A country of wonderful contrasts," wrote John Muir about Mono Lake, "hot deserts bordered by snow-laden mountains, cinder cones and ashes scattered on glacier-scoured pavement, frost and fire working together in the making of beauty." And since then, as the water level has dropped about 40 feet, towers of tufa that formed under the water have become exposed, symbolizing the unusual beauty and environmental dilemma of Mono Lake, right. JEFF GNASS

The curious chemistry of Mono Lake

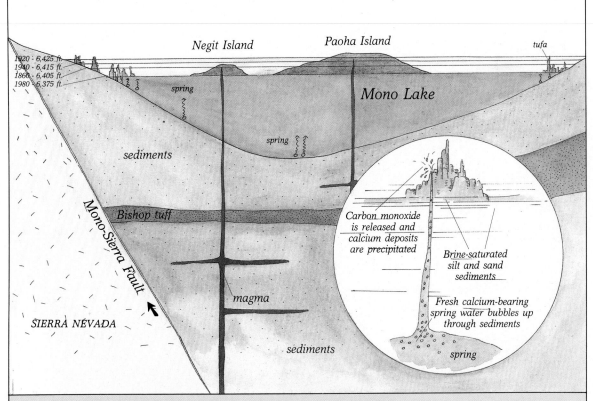

1920 · 6,425 ft.
1940 · 6,415 ft.
1860 · 6,405 ft.
1980 · 6,375 ft.

Negit Island
Paoha Island
tufa
spring
Mono Lake
spring
sediments
Mono-Sierra Fault
Bishop tuff
magma
SIERRA NEVADA
sediments
spring

Carbon monoxide is released and calcium deposits are precipitated

Brine-saturated silt and sand sediments

Fresh calcium-bearing spring water bubbles up through sediments

spring

Take an alkaline lake three times saltier than the sea and for half a million years or more percolate fresh calcium-rich spring water up from below. The calcium mixes with carbonates in the lake water and forms spires of limestone, called tufa. Drops in the level of the lake have exposed the towers and arrested their formation. Where they once grew beneath the water, they now crumble in the wind.

young here. All tallied, over one million birds use Mono Lake as a nesting ground, a feeding ground, or both.

"Mono Lake is an avian TraveLodge," says Steinhart, "the only stop for 300 miles for water-birds migrating across the Great Basin. Take it away and the flocks would have to make an 800-mile trek, from California's Salton Sea to Oregon's Lake Albert. The consequences would be felt in the Arctic tundra and on the Argentine plains."

So much for the good life at Mono Lake. Since 1941 most of the creek water that fed the inland sea has been diverted 400 miles south to Los Angeles, the largest, thirstiest, most powerful city in the nation's most populous state. By 1980 the lake was only half its original size. The surface level had dropped 46 feet. A land bridge was open to Negit Island and coyotes ravaged the gull colonies. Where 38,000 gulls had nested in 1978, only 10 nested in 1980. The salinity more than doubled and the brine shrimp numbers fell dramatically.

"You look at that and see it's a dying lake," says Vera Hansen, a long-time resident of Lee Vining, next to Mono Lake. "You can see its bones showing. When Walter and I came here on our honeymoon, it was solid wildflowers. Oh, it used to be so beautiful. Now, there's such a concentration of salts that we get this terrible air pollution. It blows up like big tornadoes, just mushrooms up into the sky. Timothy has a horse....when you'd pat him, it would come off in puffs, just like chalk." Birds used to fill the skies of Mono Lake, now it's white with dust.

The shrunken shoreline has unveiled a parched crust, but more prominent are the towers, knobs, and spires of tufa. They rise 30 feet high, broken and weathered like pagan ruins. Formed by a simple chemical reaction when spring-fed, calcium-rich groundwater mixes with alkaline lake water, the tufa precipitates out as limestone around the mouths of the springs. Their attraction is not without irony, though, since they form only

How wrong they were. Mono is the most productive, life-giving lake in California. Every May a thick soup of algae and brine shrimp erupts in the shallow, warming waters, attracting birds that descend like locusts. One fourth of the California gulls arrive to breed on Negit Island. "Myriads upon myriads of them hover over the rocks from

morning to night," wrote the naturalist J. Ross Browne in 1865, "deafening the ear with their wild screams, and the water is literally covered by them for a circle of many miles." Eighty percent of the world's eared grebes and 35 percent of the Wilson's phalaropes feast here every fall. And 10 percent of California's snowy plovers raise their

underwater and once exposed begin to crumble.

The prognosis has improved for the great inland lake—at least temporarily. Three years of heavy spring storms recently swelled the lake to levels not seen in a decade. And meanwhile, the Mono Lake Committee, with its membership approaching 10,000, stands before the Los Angeles Department of Water and Power in a David-versus-Goliath battle that may ultimately rewrite California's water laws and public trust doctrines. "Save Mono Lake," reads the blue on white bumper sticker from Crescent City to San Diego. There are more of them every year. Along with the Colorado River, Mono Lake has become the most important water issue in the western United States. *Life*, *Time*, *Newsweek*, and *National Geographic* magazines have all run feature articles on Mono Lake—no longer "the lonely tenant of the loneliest spot on Earth."

One of the greatest resource problems facing California is getting water from regions of abundance to regions of scarcity without damaging the environment. Peter Steinhart warns that, "Our cities do not end at the last freeway exit, but reach far into the wilds where they forage for fuel and water, dump their wastes, and disperse their citizens for recreation and peace of mind. The limits to things are complicated, and it sometimes takes us centuries to discover them...Mono Lake has become a landscape for our season, old, faded, forgotten by the gods, but nonetheless productive and promising if left to its true design."

Lake Tahoe State Parks and Recreation Areas

It's easy for small lakes to be beautiful. They lie in the furrows of more distant and trackless geographies, reflecting in clear waters the forests and mountains that surround them. They draw us to their quiet, lapping edges. Big lakes, on the other hand, like America's Great Lakes, also have their beauty, but their opposite shores are far away, their distances are huge and at times intimidating, their open waters are potentially violent. They feel and look like seas, not lakes.

Lake Tahoe is both. It has the mystery of something large yet the charm of something small. There is no other lake like it in all North America. Its water is (or was) as pure as a tarn's, and its forested, rocky, sandy shore wraps around it in a sometimes abrupt, sometimes gentle embrace. In 1872 Mark Twain wrote, "We plodded on...and at last the lake burst upon us—a noble sheet of blue water lifted six thousand three hundred feet above the level of the sea, and walled in by a rim of snowclad mountain peaks that towered aloft a full three thousand feet higher still!...I thought it must surely be the fairest picture the whole earth affords."

Tahoe is one of the highest lakes of its size in the world. "The Lake of the Sky," the Indians called it. It's a natural treasure everybody should see.

The National Park Service calls it "the park that got away," the lake that years ago should have been preserved in its entirety as a national park, unspoiled and uncluttered by casinos and taco stands. Developers have built their high-rise resorts on stretches of shore, mostly in Nevada on the lake's east side. To the west, though, where the shore meets the granitic shoulder of the Sierra Nevada, the State of California has established five attractive parks and recreation areas that offer almost the same Lake Tahoe that in 1844 opened the wide, startled eyes of John C. Frémont, the first white to see and record the lake.

From north to south the park units are: Kings Beach State Recreation Area, Tahoe State Recreation Area, Sugar Pine Point State Park, D.L. Bliss State Park, and Emerald Bay State Park. Visitors to all five will find a veritable banquet of recreation opportunities, including Vikingsholm in Emerald Bay and Ehrman Mansion in Sugar Pine Point state parks. Nature trails skirt the shore and cross picturesque streams broken by waterfalls and graced here and there by three species of pine—sugar, ponderosa, and Jeffrey—and white and red fir, Sierra juniper, incense cedar, black cottonwood, alder, aspen, and willow.

The wildlife isn't necessarily diverse, but it is abundant. Beneath the raucous, commonplace calls of jays and squirrels a trained ear might hear the voices of nuthatches, flickers, fly-catchers, and owls.

High altitude and cold winters have rendered Lake Tahoe less fertile than would be a lake of similar proportions elsewhere. It's not easy to warm up a body of water 22 miles long, 12 miles wide, and 1,600 feet deep. But the fishing is good, since rainbow, brown, and Mackinaw trout and Kokanee salmon (a landlocked cousin of the Pacific sockeye salmon) have been introduced.

What is the future of Lake Tahoe? Casino-related traffic jams, smog, and sewage have polluted the air and water. Anglers used to drop silver dollars in the lake and see them sparkle 100 feet down. But in 1983 the clarity was only 25 feet

deep. Dr. Charles Goldman, professor of limnology (the study of lakes) at the University of California at Davis, warns that in a few decades Lake Tahoe could become an oxygen-starved, algae-choked mess. The Lake in the Sky is, like the sky itself, turning brown. Some protective measures have been taken, but are they enough? As one observer noted, "Mark Twain saw Lake Tahoe as a 'noble sheet of blue water' because he came for the scenery, and not to catch Liberace at the cocktail show."

Clear Lake State Park

The Pomo and Lile'ek Indians say their deity Coyote dug deep into the earth, struck a spring, and filled the valley with water. But geologists say a landslide rumbled down the broad valley thousands of years ago, dammed the drainage into the Russian River, and forced the water to rise until it found a new outlet, Cache Creek, that drains eastward into the Sacramento River. In either case, Clear Lake wasn't formed by the Army Corps of Engineers.

Boats rest on calm water at the Lime Saddle Marina on Lake Oroville, left. Like other state recreation areas, Oroville offers a potpourri of water sports opportunities. JEFF GNASS

An island of water surrounded by aridity, the Salton Sea, right, is a popular recreation spot in California's southern Sonora Desert. CALIFORNIA DEPARTMENT OF PARKS AND RECREATION

It's not very deep, only 27 feet on the average and 60 feet at the maximum. But there are 100 miles of beautiful shoreline and 70 square miles of water surface—a lot of room to have a lot of fun, be it fishing, boating, picnicking, or hiking.

The Indian Nature Trail and Meadow Overlook is the quiet corner of the park. Early in the morning, when only the birds and anglers are up, a walk on this trail rekindles another time at Clear Lake—a time long ago when the Pomo and Lile'ek lived one on one with the land and the water. It's not easy to walk back thousands of years, but here in the early morning on the Indian Nature Trail it's certainly possible.

State Recreation Area Lakes and Rivers

There's no lack of opportunity for good times out here. California has almost 20 lakeside and riverside recreation areas to meet the needs of anglers, swimmers, boaters, waterskiers, scuba divers, and the like. Most of the lakes are artificial (impounded behind dams at the expense of California's free-flowing streams) and are well stocked with a variety of fish from trout to sturgeon.

Four million people a year visit Folsom Lake, just east of Sacramento. Canada geese winter here, and herons raise their young in rookeries at Anderson Island Natural Preserve. Beaver and muskrat live in the Mormon Islands wetlands. Like most of California's artificial lakes, Folsom assumes the dendritic pattern of the rivers it drowned, measuring about five times longer than it is wide.

Lake Oroville, 75 miles north of Sacramento, lies behind the highest earthfill dam in the United States. An impressive visitor center on Kelly Ridge has displays on water projects and natural and cultural history. Far up the Middle Fork of the Feather River, within a quarter mile of boat access during high water, is 640-foot Feather Falls. Boat-in campsites are spread along the lake's 167 miles of shoreline.

Lake Perris, 11 miles southeast of Riverside, boasts the first regional Indian museum (several more are planned) within the California State Park System. It depicts the complex societies and sophisticated resourcefulness of the Cahuilla, Chemehuevi, Cupeño, Luiseño, Serrano, and Vanyume peoples, and concentrates on three different time periods: "Adapting to a Desert Homeland," "Surviving a Century of Destruction," and "Renewing the Heritage." A horse trail and bike trail each circle the lake, and rock climbers can sharpen their skills on Big Rock at the southern end of the lake.

Millerton Lake, 20 miles northeast of Fresno, is in the geographical heart of California. Like most of the state's recreational lakes, it can accommodate over 1,000 boats at a time, provided everyone follows the rules. Beneath the water is the original site of Camp Barbour, where the Mariposa Indian War ended in 1851. A significant piece of the area's gold rush history was preserved when the old Millerton County Courthouse (built in 1867) was dismantled in 1941 and moved to its present site next to Friant Dam.

Way down in the state's southeast corner are Salton Sea and Picacho state recreation areas. Both are offspring of the once mighty Colorado River, but that's where their similarities end. The Salton Sea formed in 1905 when irrigation floodgates on the Colorado broke near Yuma, Arizona, and drained for two years into the Salton Sink, flooding homes, farmlands, and desert. The Bureau of Land Management reported that "technology has merely introduced a temporary hiatus in the normal course of events." With rainfall and irrigation drainoff balancing evaporation, the lake has stabilized at 35 miles long, 15 miles wide, and an average depth of only 20 feet. Migratory birds rely heavily on the Salton Sea; over 350 species have been recorded. Picacho provides access to 55 miles of the gently curving Colorado River between Parker and Imperial dams. The old gold-mining town of Picacho is flooded, but the mill sites remain. Twenty-five hundred people lived here at the turn of the century, and an estimated $14 million worth of gold was recovered. Things are quieter now. Boaters get the feeling that they've got the whole river to themselves.

A more popular desert blue jewel is Silverwood Lake, 30 miles north of San Bernardino. Surrounded by the San Bernardino National Forest, it supports 130 species of birds, plus a half dozen species of sport fish that thrive in the brushy areas left uncleared when the lake was created. Water travels over 400 miles to reach this point then drops a thousand feet through a nearly vertical pipeline to provide hydroelectric power and drinking water for southern California.

Other recreation lakes include San Luis and Bethany reservoirs along the California Aqueduct Bike Trail, Benbow Lake with its annual Shakespeare Festival, Lakes Earl and Talawa for visitors wishing to find peace and quiet and birds in a nondeveloped marshland, Lake Del Valle with its tour boat, and Lake Elsinore and Castaic Lake for heat-weary southern Californians who want to escape from the city without having to drive long distances.

Many lakes for many purposes for many people. They quench our thirst, water our lands, control flooding, turn turbines, create habitat, offer an education, and provide for a tremendous amount of outdoor recreation. They are rare jewels indeed that can do all that. ∎

The lonely, lovely desert

"A grim wasteland," people called it. "The Mojave?" an old cowboy quipped. "That ain't no place to be. Everything out there sticks, stings, or stinks." Some folks said it was a place of death, not life. Sun-bleached bones and vultures. No wonder the last blank spots on the maps of California were in the Mojave Desert.

All places have their secrets, but none keeps them so well as deserts. Water, for example, leaves its signature everywhere—in washes, playas, and canyons—yet the water itself is hard to find. But it's out there. The bighorn sheep know where it is, so do the coyotes.

There are two desert regions in California—the Mojave and the Colorado. The Mojave Desert is also called the upper desert because its elevation ranges from below sea level in Death Valley to 4,500 feet. It extends from the western end of Antelope Valley northeast to Death Valley and south to the Riverside County line. Below it is the lower or Colorado Desert, part of the Sonora Desert which extends east into Arizona and south into Mexico. The elevation here ranges from below sea level to 2,000 feet, and it's considerably hotter and drier than the Mojave.

California has taken choice pockets of desert lands and set them aside as state parks. They are worlds of canyons, cacti, and coyotes and in the case of the Providence Mountains, caverns, too. Most of these parks are less than three hours away from half of California's population. Time slows down in places like Anza-Borrego and Red Rock Canyon. Preoccupations with one-hour photo, 24-hour Martinizing, and 10-minute parking wash away in the cool morning breeze. There's just daytime and nighttime, dusk and dawn. That's the magic of the lonely, lovely desert. Beyond the old prejudices, we discover the so-called "grim wasteland" is actually a tremendous teacher.

Anza-Borrego Desert State Park

Anza-Borrego, just east of San Diego, used to be country to get through, now it's a place to go to. At 600,000 acres, it's the largest state park in the contiguous United States. All other units combined

Shy denizens of the arid mountains, desert bighorn sheep, below, have fallen in numbers the past hundred years due to poaching, habitat loss, and disease. Because of its immense size and ruggedness, Anza-Borrego Desert State Park remains a pristine stronghold of the wild sheep.
RICK McINTYRE

The desert tortoise (Gopherus agassizi), below, lives throughout the Mojave and Colorado deserts of California. In spite of thick, protective shells, desert tortoises are dormant in both winter and the heat of summer when adverse temperatures are common, and they spend the time in burrows, which they dig in wash banks and other suitable terrain. RICK McINTYRE

California fan palms (Washingtonia filifera) stand next to a flowering ocotillo in the Southwest Grove in Anza-Borrego Desert State Park, right. This is the only species of native palm in the western United States and is the largest of the true desert palms, attaining 80 feet in height. The dying leaves of the previous year bend downward in an insulating mat that protects the tree from extreme summer heat.
LARRY ULRICH

From Font's Point, at 1,294 feet above sea level, visitors get a breathtaking view of the Borrego Badlands, far left, and beyond to the trail Juan Bautista de Anza blazed from Mexico to California in the 1770s. Font's Point honors Father Pedro Font, scribe of the second Anza expedition in 1775. RICK McINTYRE

Photography, left, is a favorite pastime (and profession) in the desert in the spring, especially in the first and last hours of the day when the sun casts rich light across the sky and through the spines of cacti. PAT O'HARA

in the California State Park System would fit into Anza-Borrego. It's a pristine ecosystem, a place that becomes more and more valuable in an increasingly populated and automated world. Anza-Borrego is for people, but it also belongs to the wild plants and animals that came long before you and I.

The habitats range from desert washes with palo verde, indigo bush, and burroweed, up 6,000 feet to pinyon, juniper, scrub oak, sumac, and mountain mahogany. The greater Anza-Borrego area has 600 species of plants and 350 species of birds, mammals, and reptiles. It's a big, beautiful, encyclopedic place.

Looking in any direction from the Santa Rosa Mountains, the highest peaks in the park, one sees an eroded, treeless land with rock strata folded, faulted, and turned on end. The canyons open like

rock-ribbed vaults, and the mountains rise along razor-backed ridges. In the Vallecito-Fish Creek-Carrizo area are over 100 species of fossil animals, representing what has been called "one of the most remarkably complete sequences of animal life to be found anywhere in the world." Textbook examples of erosion stand juxtaposed to textbook examples of deposition. The rocks right here might be 500 times older than those over there.

The San Andreas Fault runs just to the east and is responsible for a multimillion-year chronology of upheaval. There are mountains capped with ancient coral and oyster reefs. Beneath those are volcanic hills, and farther down still are sand dunes and sedimentary canyons sired and cut by the wind.

The granitic pluton of Borrego Mountain rises in steep counterpoint to the valley-bottom playa

clays patterned like the carapace of a desert tortoise. There is no end to it all. Geology students learn more here in a week than in three months back in the classroom.

Down in the shaded canyon areas are palm groves filled with orioles, buntings, hummingbirds, verdins, and the people who find endless delight in watching them.

Some of the birds stay year-round, but most migrate through, like the people. Up on a rocky ledge might be the remnants of a bighorn sheep killed by a mountain lion, or the bones of ancient Yuha Man who lived here thousands of years ago when savannah-type environments surrounded the shores of Pleistocene lakes.

Spring in Anza-Borrego has to be seen to be believed. Brittle bush washes the mountainsides yellow with its flowers. Cactus "forests" open their showy blossoms in reds, purples, creams, golds, and mandarins. Stalks of the great agaves, having waited a lifetime to bloom, rise 20 feet into the sky, burst open, and attract the secret comings and goings of nocturnal pollinators. And the ocotillo, the rose of the desert, breaks into jubilant red flowers at the tips of its long, thorny branches. Millions of tiny but brilliant blossoms, some belonging to plants that may not have flowered for years, sparkle like constellations across the desert floor. The telephone rings off the wall in the visitor center. People from Merced, Malibu, or Manhattan wonder if the whispering bells are blooming. Or ghost flowers? Or sand verbena? "I've been coming here for over thirty years," an

The great desert wildflower scoop

It's difficult to predict from one spring to the next when the California deserts will bloom brightest. Depending on temperature and the amount of rainfall, the flowers might peak as early as March one year or as late as May the next. So the question arises, "When is the best time to go?" The staff at Anza-Borrego Desert State Park has a solution.

Every winter hundreds of wildflower enthusiasts send self-addressed stamped postcards to the park with messages like "The Anza-Borrego Desert wildflowers will probably be at their best in one week" or "The wildflowers are excellent now, come to Anza-Borrego as soon as possible." The park staff watches the flowers and sends the cards out at the appropriate times.

In lieu of sending a postcard, visitors often telephone the park at (619) 767-5311 and ask about the flowers. Either way, the staff at Anza-Borrego dedicates itself to informing the public of the spring desert colors. It's a spectacular show, and they don't want anyone to miss it.

The blossom of a beavertail cactus (Opuntia basilaris), above. One of the most common cati, its flowering sets the desert ablaze in bright red. KIM HEACOX

An arc of yellow blossoms catches the late afternoon light atop a barrel cactus (Echinocactus acanthodes), far left. This cylindrical cactus can grow to heights of nine feet, although two to four feet is most common. It tends to lean in the direction of the greatest light. KIM HEACOX

Like roses surrounded by thorns, three blossoms of a hedgehog cactus (Echinocereus engelmanii), left, flower amid a sea of spines. Although rare when compared with most other species of California's cacti, the hedgehog is nevertheless considered by many cactus connoisseurs to be the most beautiful. KIM HEACOX

Halos of light surround jumping cholla (Opuntia bigelovii) beneath a temperamental sky in Mason Valley, left. The variety in the background, hoffmannii, is found only in Anza-Borrego Desert State Park. BILL EVARTS

old man says. His face is the color of dried galleta grass, and his hands the texture of granite. But his smile is soft and his voice sincere. "Those who think the desert is a hot, dry, dreary place haven't seen Anza-Borrego in the spring."

They haven't seen Anza-Borrego, period. A desert in spring is a landscape in all its finery, but the picture becomes more subtle during the rest of the year. Shadow play lingers in the topography. The textures of playa, rock, and bone become vivid.

The sky makes its own mountains when winter storms and summer thunderheads roll across Anza-Borrego. The heat is still here; it can kill a man. But with a change of light, a calling wren, or a sudden rainstorm, Anza-Borrego becomes a beautiful and poetic place. Even the names are poetic: Quartz Vein Wash, Hapaha Flat, Carrizo Badlands, Glorietta Canyon, Montezuma Grade, Narrows Earth Trail, Arroyo Salado, and Canyon Sin Nombre (Canyon with No Name).

The most curious name, though, and probably the most fitting is Anza-Borrego. It hybridizes quintessential elements of the park's human and natural history: Anza, the brilliant Spanish explorer who twice led expeditions through the heart of the park; and borrego, the Spanish term for the desert bighorn sheep, the secretive, elusive animal that imparts a wilderness flavor to any land it inhabits.

Juan Bautista de Anza, like his grandfather and father before him, was commander of the presidio at Tubac (in southern Arizona) and governor of the province of Sonora. But Juan Bautista III would bring even greater honor to his family name.

In 1773 he proposed that an overland immigration and supply route be opened between northern Mexico and California. It was exactly what the viceroy in Mexico City wanted. California had 5 missions then, but only 61 soldiers and 11 padres. Supply ships were sporadic. Spanish women and children were rare. "Near starvation," read one account, "was a way of life" in California. The 39-year-old Anza had his work cut out for him.

Striking out across terra incognita, he led 20 volunteers and a few dozen head of cattle through what are now Ocotillo Wells and Anza-Borrego parks. They stopped at Harper's Well and San Gregorio (Borrego Springs) before continuing through Coyote Canyon and over San Carlos Pass. They arrived at Mission San Gabriel in late March 1774, and by May the fleet-footed Anza was back in Mexico City to report on his success.

His trail now blazed, Anza mounted an ambitious expedition of 1,000 animals and 240 people (most of them women and children, plus a few soldiers and three friars). It was a long slow trek through terrible daytime heat and bitter nighttime cold. But these were high-spirited colonists walking to a brighter future. Anza called them *pobladores*, or populators. On Christmas Eve 1775, with the hardest terrain behind them, the expedition sang and danced after a woman gave birth to a son in Coyote Canyon. The Spanish population of California nearly doubled when Anza's expedition arrived at Mission San Gabriel in early January 1776. And by the end of the eighteenth century, half the white citizens and most of the livestock in California would be veterans of Anza's famous trail.

A much different migration came through Anza-Borrego in November 1846, when Kit Carson led General Stephen Kearny and his 100 dragoons, more properly known as the U.S. Army of the West, into California to control Californio insurgents during the Mexican-American War. They crossed Anza's path in Coyote Wash (a couple miles north of present-day Plaster City) and continued through the Carrizo corridor along Vallecito Creek to Mason Valley, Box Canyon, and San Felipe Wash. It was one of the most difficult treks ever endured by the American military on its own soil. Even the indefatigable Carson cursed the trail. So weary and poorly provisioned were the soldiers after the trek that they stumbled into the Californios at San Pasqual and suffered serious

losses at what is now San Pasqual Battlefield State Historic Park.

A month behind Carson and Kearny came the famous Mormon Battalion, assigned to blaze a year-round wagon trail to California. It was easier said than done. The exhausted, shoeless men had to hack with axes at the rocks in Box Canyon and disassemble some of the wagons to get through. Although the route seemed absurd at the time, two years later it was busy with California-bound '49ers who preferred to take their chances with the Colorado Desert heat rather than with the snows of the Sierra Nevada, the threat of yellow fever in Panama, or the possibility of shipwreck around the Horn. Cartographers called the new route the Southern Emigrant Trail, but those who had been there called it *Jornada del Muerto*—the Journey of Death. It was easy to find; they just followed the bleached bones of horses, cattle, and people.

Conditions improved in the 1850s when the San Diego Overland Mail Line and the Butterfield Overland Mail Line carried passengers and mail from the midwest to California. It took 30 days to go from St. Louis to Los Angeles. There are ghosts from those days, so the local people say. Four bandits robbed a stage of $65,000 between the Carrizo and Vallecito stations. The stage driver was killed as were two of the bandits. But a ghost stage continued on its way and people still hear it on the trail today. The two remaining bandits buried the loot before they shot and killed each other over the typical "who gets how much" argument. Apparently, the money is still buried out there and anyone who happens to approach it sees a ghost of the leader's horse as it rears up and gallops across the land, erasing all traces of the treasure as it goes.

Another ghost is that of a young, beautiful woman who fell ill on the stage and died in Vallecito. In her suitcase was the wedding gown she was to have worn in Sacramento. She was buried in her gown, and so legend says, she rises from her grave now and then to wander about the old Vallecito Station.

The Civil War and the advent of the railroads closed down the old stagecoach lines through Anza-Borrego. All that remained was an epitaph of ghosts and of wagon ruts etched into the rock. Soon thereafter homesteaders began to arrive with their families and cattle. The living was never bountiful, but it was enough.

Anza-Borrego Desert State Park provides an opportunity to meet the desert on its own terms. We must play by the desert's rules and learn a valuable humility. Such is the power of Anza-Borrego. It's a place of nameless mountains and trackless valleys that reminds us that before we belonged to cities and nations, we belonged to the earth.

Providence Mountains State Recreation Area

The ultimate desert rat goes to Providence Mountains State Recreation Area. Sequestered in a solitary haunt in the middle of nowhere, 80 miles east of Barstow, it is the most isolated unit in the California State Park System. Sheer curiosity is reason enough to visit, and quiet beauty is reason enough to stay. These mountains are loaded with surprises, both above and below the ground.

On clear days the rising sun breaks over Arizona, hits the Providence Mountains, and washes amber light down the 7,000-foot limestone and rhyolite

Dressed in an interplay of sunlight and shadow, the Providence Mountains break an angry sky in the desert outback of southeast California. Beneath these limestone and rhyolite peaks lay the Mitchell Caverns, the main attraction at Providence Mountains State Recreation Area. The surrounding lowlands support a variety of plantlife, including these robust barrel cacti.
KAZ HAGIWARA

vertebrae of Edgar and Fountain peaks, highest points in the recreation area. Mesas, hills, sand dunes, and cinder cones cover the foothills with a potpourri of shapes, colors, and rock types. The park headquarters and visitor's center lie tucked like a chuckwalla into the rocks at 4,300 feet, a relatively cool and comfortable elevation compared with the hot surrounding basins.

Some of the oldest rocks in the Mojave Desert—outcrops of granite and gneisss formed some two billion years ago—are exposed in the slopes just below park headquarters. A tough lamina of life covers the baked earth of the Providence Mountains, and the 1.5-mile-long Mary Beal Nature Trail is a good introduction to many of the area's landforms and life forms.

The biggest attraction, however, is what lies beneath it all: the Mitchell Caverns Natural Preserve. Jack Mitchell, a miner and loner, found the caves while prospecting for silver in l929. They had been previously discovered, but Mitchell built his life around them and with his wife, Ida, provided tours and on-site food and lodging. He renamed the caves Tecopa, after a Shoshonean chief, and El Pakiva, the Devil's House.

Formed over the last 12 million years as weak acidic rainwater percolated through limestone bedrock, the caves today are filled with intricate calcite formations. Stalactites hang from the ceiling and stalagmites stand on the floor. These dripstone formations have stopped growing since the rainfall has decreased and the climate has warmed over the last 10,000 years.

Although nature has a way of creating holes like caves, valleys, and canyons, she also works ceaselessly at filling them. Mitchell Caverns are

These deeply eroded badlands in Red Rock Canyon State Park hold fossil evidence of the animals—horses, camels, large carnivores, rabbits, rodents, and lizards—that once throve here when the Mojave Desert had a more hospitable climate.
CARR CLIFTON

already filling with dust, and as earthquakes rattle the Providence Mountains and surface erosion continues, the caverns will eventually collapse. But all this will happen in another time, in desert time, after maybe a hundred or a thousand of our generations have come and gone.

Red Rock Canyon State Park

Remember John Wayne riding horseback and looking for bad guys in the red-rock canyons of the Old West? A minute later he would be galloping past tall, bleached-white cliffs and chocolate-brown boulders. This was no movie set, nor was it the cinnabar canyon country of the Colorado Plateau. It was Red Rock Canyon State Recreation Area on Highway 14 near Mojave, a piece of southern Utah grafted onto California.

For every recreation seeker who visits Red Rock Canyon, at least 1,000 drive right past it. Skiers on their way to Mammoth, hikers headed for the Sierra Nevada, or desert rats off to Death Valley, they're all going somewhere else. But those who stop and snoop around the red sedimentary rocks discover a strangely beautiful world, a land right out of the movies. And they have it all to themselves.

College geology field classes make annual treks to Red Rock Canyon to study the sediments of a Pliocene lake bed and the intermittent capstones of basalt, sandstone, and tuff. Fossil evidence suggests that a few million years ago the lakeshore was where the canyon is now. Tall grasses covered the land then, and along the shore walked horses, camels, antelopes, saber-toothed cats, wolves, mastodons, and two species of rhinoceroses.

Today, after thousands of years of warmer temperatures and less precipitation, the baked land is home to mice, rabbits, squirrels, coyotes, bats, lizards, and snakes. The ancient lake and savannah have become a desert canyon, lifeless at first glance but filled with life upon closer inspection.

A spring rain squall and early morning light create a rainbow behind a flowering ocotillo (Fouquieria splendens) in Anza-Borrego Desert State Park. Leafless and seemingly lifeless most of the year, the ocotillo develops green branches and scarlet blossoms when its widespread, shallow root system collects enough moisture. Borrego Valley and the mouth of Coyote Canyon are excellent areas to observe large concentrations of ocotillo. PAT O'HARA

Within the recreation area there are two natural preserves: Red Cliffs and Hagen Canyon. As the sun sets, an ethereal light remains, as if the rocks themselves were aglow. A landscape photographer stood in the warm twilight and summed up a common reaction to the desert. He peered over his camera and said, "What an incredible place; I could kick myself for not coming here sooner." What he deserved, though, was a pat on the back for coming here at all.

Saddleback Butte State Park

During the fifties as Los Angeles and its northern satellites spread outward, public concern mounted over saving nearby pockets of pristine desert before they were dissected by roads, fences, and subdivisions. Saddleback Butte State Park was thus established on the edge of the Mojave Desert in 1960.

The butte is a weathered spur of granite rising a thousand feet above the broad alluvial fan of Antelope Valley. Visitors hike to the top along a half-mile trail beginning at the family camp-ground. The biggest attractions, though, are the forests of Joshua trees. A member of the lily family and a close relative of yuccas, the Joshua tree has come to symbolize the Mojave Desert much as the giant saguaro cactus symbolizes Arizona's Sonora Desert. Early pioneers saw in its branches a likeness to the supplicating arms of the prophet Joshua pointing with his spear to the city of Ai.

The human story here is short. There was no water, so there were no people. The Indians followed the Mojave River and lived in the Tehachapi Mountains to the north and west, or in the San Gabriels to the south. But Saddleback Butte made a good hideout for rebels fleeing from soldiers out of Fort Tejon. The arrival of the railroad in the 1870s had strong ecological repercussions as the area's thousands of pronghorn antelope were unable to cross the tracks to good pasture on the other side. Within a few years the entire population died.

Today, Antelope Valley has no antelope, but it has new irrigation technologies that suck water out of the ground to wet alfalfa and other crops. It has borax mines that dig ceaselessly at the land, and it has post-World War II defense and aerospace industries that have grown like cheat-grass.

One of the few places that hasn't changed is Saddleback Butte and its surrounding forests of Joshua trees. If what Henry David Thoreau said is true, that "a man is rich in proportion to the number of things he can afford to let alone," then Saddleback Butte State Park was indeed created by the rich. It pays all of us back in large dividends.

The desert rewards patience. It has great things to teach us, but only when we slow down, take it easy, and meet the land on its own terms. Author-naturalist Barry Lopez writes, "The faster the eye is moving the fewer things it will see." California's desert state parks beg us to slow down. So what's the hurry? When we come to appreciate space as much as we are obsessed with time, and when we realize that there is more to life than increasing its speed, we look down to see our feet firmly planted in the baked earth of the deserts of California. ∎

Prickly pear cactus, widely distributed in southern California, brings seasonal beauty and color to the desert. The fruit of many species of prickly pear cactus is quite tasty and can be eaten raw or cooked, but be careful of the spines. ED COOPER

Ecological islands

All parks are islands. Hemmed in by different habitats and topography or by encroaching civilization, they stand apart as refuges for the organisms living there. To waterfowl, a pond or lake is an island surrounded by land. The same is true for a salamander restricted to a moist, forested furrow enclosed by dry chaparral. To deer, a valley of brushland and forest is a natural sanctuary cloistered by mountains, but the very ridges and peaks of those mountains are in turn island homes to alpine plants and animals.

Some parks are mere vestiges of habitats that once covered huge areas. They represent the last remaining islands of once great worlds of native plants and wildlife long since lost to agriculture, logging, and shopping centers. The Tule Elk and Antelope Valley Poppy state reserves are good examples.

The eye finds aesthetic value in these parks as well. McArthur-Burney Falls is not necessarily a rich wildlife area, but its scenic beauty is without peer. And Mount Diablo offers some of the greatest vistas in the state.

This chapter is a mélange, then, a brief brush stroke to remind us of the rich pockets of habitat and scenery that make California far too precious to compromise. Dozens upon dozens of state parks, reserves, natural preserves, and wildernesses easily qualify for this chapter, but there isn't enough room to discuss them all. Many, in fact, are in other chapters illustrating stronger themes. Take a lifetime to find them, and give a lifetime to protecting them. It will be a partnership filled with gratification.

Tule Elk State Reserve

"At times we saw bands of elk, deer, and antelope in such numbers that they actually darkened the plains for miles and looked in the distance like great herds of cattle," wrote pioneer Edward Bosqui about California's Central Valley in 1850.

By all accounts, the tule elk was to California what the bison was to the North American plains. Ranging from the north-central Sacramento Valley to the Tehachapi Mountains and from the Sierra Nevada foothills to the Coast Ranges, they formed herds of 40 to 2,000 animals across the grass and oak savannahs. With antelope and deer and a few

*Tule elk (***Cervus elaphus nannodes***), left, graze on their reserve in the San Joaquin Valley, near the intersection of I-5 and the Stockdale Road. Probably the most exciting time to view them is during the fall rut when bulls bugle and lock antlers fighting over the rights to mate with cows.* CALIFORNIA DEPARTMENT OF PARKS AND RECREATION

Boulders of basalt glisten beneath Burney Falls, right, in the volcanic country of northern California. Summer is the most popular time to visit McArthur-Burney Falls Memorial State Park, when the curtain of water offers a cool respite from the surrounding heat. CARR CLIFTON

predatory bears, mountain lions, and coyotes, the tule elk formed the focal point of a great sea of wildlife. It was a California Serengeti.

In less than 20 years it was gone.

Carried on the boots of the early Spaniards were the seeds of aggressive annual grasses that spread across the valley and displaced the perennial bunch grasses valuable to the elk. Professional hunters began killing 3,000 per year for the hide and tallow trade. Fences crept across the land. The gold rush raised the value of a cow from $2 to $35, ranching boomed, and the elk were suddenly regarded as a competitive nuisance. In two years the Sacramento Valley population was decimated. Farther south, the elk retreated into the bulrushes, or tules (hence their name), of the San Joaquin River Delta. In 1863 hunters boasted of killing the last cow and calf. Some elk did survive, however, in the marshes between Buena Vista and Tulare lakes. They seemed safe until farmers diked and drained the land to make it more suitable for agriculture. And so it came to pass. Of the tens of thousands of tule elk that had once thrived in California, only a few remained.

It's a sad legacy the history books tend to ignore. Tule Elk State Reserve, 27 miles west of Bakersfield off Interstate 5, is the last, best hope for the survival of a noble animal. The habitat is not natural, and the California Department of Parks and Recreation hopes to someday acquire a larger, more natural reserve for the elk. In the meantime, the elk live in a microcosm of their former world, rutting every fall, calving every spring, and wallowing in artificial ponds every summer. The sight isn't what it used to be, but it's something every Californian should see.

McArthur-Burney Falls Memorial State Park

Ask someone who's familiar with California's state parks to sum up the system in one representative unit (an unfair question in the first place),

A stately black oak shades the edge of a meadow in Cuyamaca Rancho State Park, 40 miles east of San Diego. The Indians who lived here for 7,000 years called the area Ah-ha-Kwe-ah-mac, "the place where it rains." From the summit of the park, at 6,512 feet atop Cuyamaca Peak, one can see Anza-Borrego Desert State Park to the east and the Pacific Coast to the west, while falling away below is a world of pine and oak forests, broad meadows, and cool streams. BILL EVARTS

and sooner or later he'll say McArthur-Burney Falls. Never heard of it? Granted, it's not big, it's not famous, and, lying some 70 miles northeast of Redding, it's not near a major population center.

Burney Falls, the centerpiece of the park, is one of nature's best kept secrets in California. President Theodore Roosevelt called it the eighth wonder of the world.

The park straddles the ragged edge of two major geologic provinces: the southern Cascade Range and the Modoc Plateau. This is volcano country. Mount Shasta lies just to the north; Mount Lassen to the south.

For at least 20 million years this land has cracked open to erupt with countless volcanic mudflows and basalt and andesite lavas. Erosion-resistant basalt forms the capstone that intersects Burney Creek and forces it into a spectacular 129-foot twin waterfall. Curtains of smaller waterfalls fed by underground streams pour out of the surrounding cliffs year-round, creating a broad wall of tumbling water—"California's Niagara."

John and Catherine McArthur settled in this area

in 1869. Their son, Frank, became concerned that dams built on the Pit River would flood Burney Falls. In 1922 he deeded 160 acres (including the falls) to the State of California for future protection and public use.

Cuyamaca Rancho State Park

If not for Anza-Borrego Desert State Park looming 25 times larger to the east, Cuyamaca Rancho would probably bask in greater popularity. Perhaps there's a blessing in that. Anza-Borrego gets most of the attention, but Cuyamaca Rancho gets most of the rain. It's the mountains of this quiet, beautiful, and relatively unpeopled park that steal precipitation and leave the Anza-Borrego Desert hot and dry. The average elevation exceeds 4,000 feet, crowned by Cuyamaca Peak at 6,512 feet on the western boundary.

Half of the park's 25,000 acres are designated wilderness—closed to all vehicles, even bicycles. Trails wind through stands of Coulter, sugar, ponderosa, and Jeffrey pines, plus incense cedar, white fir, and an equally abundant variety of

April softens the desert with flowering yucca, brittle bush, and beavertail cactus, yet winter lingers on the snowy, 10,804-foot summit of Mount San Jacinto. Uncluttered by picnic tables, trash containers, toilet facilities, roads, and other "conveniences," the mountain is a state wilderness (the first established in California) where visitors are required to pack out everything they pack in. ED COOPER

deciduous trees. Over 100 species of birds have been recorded in the park.

The natural history of the area mirrors an equally vibrant human history, from the days when Governor Pio Pico first granted Rancho Cuyamaca to Augustin Olverra in 1845, through times of placer and hard-rock mining (the Stonewall Mine yielded over $2 million in gold), and finally to 1933 when Mr. and Mrs. Ralph Dyar sold the land to the state for half its appraised value.

The park is a well-kept secret of forests and cool air in the hot, southernmost reaches of California. "Cuyamaca Rancho?" people say. "Never heard of it." Those who have been there like to keep it that way.

Mount San Jacinto State Park and State Wilderness

People around San Bernardino call it "San Jack" or just "the mountain." They look out their kitchen windows and say, "Winter's coming, there's snow on the mountain." Or they meet newcomers to the area and ask, "You been up yet? It's a great view." A white, snow-capped reprieve from a hot, dry land, it reminds them that other worlds are right out their back door. Come July in the lower desert, that's a tremendous reassurance.

At 10,804 feet, Mount San Jacinto rises from Sonoran to alpine life zones. It's the highest point in the California State Park System. Park rangers are proud of that and also that San Jacinto was the first state wilderness. Created in 1937, it was a giant step forward for California. Its brochure reads, "When you're hiking the San Jacinto Wilderness, don't expect picnic tables, trash containers, toilet facilities, roads, or other conveniences. Be prepared for the unexpected. The weather can change suddenly, and the Wilderness

has claimed several lives. Though you enter the Wilderness at your own risk, and must be prepared to take care of yourself, in return you will find unspoiled vistas, solitude, and a chance to escape the frantic pace of civilization." All of that less than three hours away from half of California's population.

The aerial tram below is an abrupt contrast. It runs from 2,643 feet in Chino Canyon, near Palm Springs, up to a restaurant and gift shop at Mountain Station, elevation 8,516 feet. Six million people have taken the tram since it opened in 1963. Promoters call it a triumph; wilderness advocates call it a travesty. Said one environmentalist, "You appreciate a view like this a hundred times more when you pay for it out of your heart, not out of your wallet."

Mount Diablo State Park

"It's the sides of the mountain which sustain life," writes Robert Pirsig, "not the top." If it wasn't Mount Diablo that inspired Pirsig's words, it easily could have been. Wrapped in a shawl of oak woodland, grassland, and chaparral, and stitched here and there with pine and maple, this is a mountain ripe with native vegetation. Yet most visitors head straight for the summit.

In *California Mountain Ranges* (Volume 1 in the California Geographic Series), Russell B. Hill writes, "The view from Mount Diablo, with an

A textbook example of central California oak woodland covers the slopes of Mount Diablo, left, a short distance east of San Francisco Bay. Grassland and chaparral mix with the oak and add to the over 400 species of plants within the park's nearly 16,000 acres. Summers are hot and dry here, and winters mild, but every so often a storm crowns Mount Diablo with snow so that people from the Bay Area have to drive up to rub the stuff between their fingers to make sure it's real. CARR CLIFTON

elevation of only 3,849 feet, encompasses more than 40,000 square miles. The peak essentially stands alone on the edge of the great Central Valley. Only Africa's Mount Kilimanjaro, five times higher, surveys more."

Oldtimers say that on clear days (the best are in winter and early spring after storms blow away the smog) the view reaches 200 miles into 35 of California's 58 counties. Two-thirds of California was surveyed from atop Mount Diablo, as well as parts of Oregon and Nevada. With steady hands and a good pair of binoculars one might see Mount Lassen and a refracted image of Mount Shasta to the north, Half Dome in Yosemite Valley to the east, Lick Observatory on Mount Hamilton to the south, and the Farallon Islands 28 miles beyond the Golden Gate to the west.

Yet the most spectacular view might be right at your feet—Mount Diablo itself. Scattered about are unusual sandstone formations, small caves, abundant wildlife, and some well-preserved fossils. Hiking trails wander out to North Peak and Eagle Peak and descend into canyons and flats on all sides of the mountain.

Out beyond Mounts San Jacinto and Diablo are other islands in the sky in California's state park system—Castle Crags, Mount Tamalpais, and Fremont Peak among them.

At Castle Crags, just south of Mount Shasta, spires of teeth-like granite break the horizon. One of the rock formations strongly resembles Yosemite's Half Dome. The park has 18 miles of trails, including a portion of the Pacific Crest Trail.

Mount Tamalpais, the crown of Marin County, climbs above the Golden Gate north of San Francisco. Like Mount Diablo, it affords spectacular views of the Bay Area, plus 30 miles of hiking trails. Mount Tamalpais hosts more than a hundred different species of wildflowers, including blue lupine, poppies, Douglas iris, and blue-eyed grass, with displays especially dazzling in March and April.

South of the Bay Area, near Hollister (and San Juan Bautista State Historic Park), is Fremont Peak (3,171 feet). The name is ironic, since John C. Frémont, regarded by many historians as a nearly pathologically vain man, planted the Stars and Stripes there in 1846, strafed the Mexican Army with empty rhetoric, then stole away at night and retreated into Oregon. Years later, John Steinbeck spent some of his finest boyhood days exploring the grasslands atop Fremont Peak where he found the cannonballs and old bayonets of bygone times.

The island analogy can easily extend to forested parks that lie above surrounding agricultural fields. Visitors in California's wine country, for example, will find three attractive state parks: Bothe-Napa Valley, Annadel, and Sugarloaf Ridge. Bothe-Napa Valley boasts a handsome blend of evergreen and deciduous trees. Annadel, its brochure says, is a "wilderness at your doorstep," only 60 miles from San Francisco, with "35 miles of trails in nearly 5,000 acres of rolling hills, intermittent streams, meadows, and woodland unmarred by modern intrusions." Sugarloaf Ridge, equally enticing, is a favorite haunt of wildflower buffs.

The islands go on and on—islands of habitat and islands of history. What unit in the California State Park System is not an island? Isolated and rare in a runaway world, they become valuable far beyond dollars, pictures, or words. We escape into them and emerge with a new sense of hope. ∎

Let the good times roll

Back in the early seventies people in the town of Hollister were upset. Motorcycles, three-wheel vehicles, jeeps, and dune buggies were zipping across their farms and ranches and down the streets. "Those crazy kids come down here from San Jose and ride all over the damn place," one disgruntled farmer said. "They chew up good land. And now the state wants to make a park for them right here next to Hollister. It's nuts."

What a surprise, then, when Hollister Hills State Vehicular Recreation Area (SVRA) was established and everybody was happy, even the farmers. "Well," one said, "it's worked out just fine. Those kids have a lot of fun out there. They've got their territory and we've got ours. They're not riding out on the farms and ranches and highways anymore. I think it's great."

For the new recreation area, the state carefully selected land heavily used by off-highway vehicles.

Today, Hollister Hills SVRA is 3,300 acres of oak woodlands and grassy coastal foothills. A maze of roads wraps through the area with designated sites for motorcycles, 4-wheel-drives, and all-terrain vehicles (ATVs).

Hollister Hills SVRA is a hallmark of resource management where strictly enforced rules maintain the area's integrity. A quarter of a million dollars has been spent on trail rehabilitation. Some of the trails have been closed for revegetation, allowing the land to heal, while others have been rerouted to minimize soil erosion.

Mike Bishop, an off-road vehicle advocate, says, "Many people throughout the country feel these vehicles are the antithesis of parks and recreation. They wonder, 'Why does California spend so much time and money to accommodate these potentially destructive vehicles?' The answer is in our title: Parks and *Recreation*. Off-highway ve-

hicles are a legitimate form of recreation."

In 1971 an environmentalist and an off-road enthusiast decided it would be to everyone's benefit to create specific areas for off-highway vehicles. It was a major accomplishment in the cooperation of two opposing groups. While off-roading became concentrated, adjacent lands would remain untracked.

Eleven years later the Off-Highway Division split from the Department of Parks and Recreation and created its own seven-member commission. Three of the commissioners are appointed by the governor, two by the state senate, and two by the state assembly. All serve for four-year terms. Their goals and objectives reflect an enlightened attitude towards off-highway vehicle use in California.

California has spent nearly $50 million over the last two decades on the planning, acquisition, and development of its six state vehicular recreation areas: Pismo Dunes, Hungry Valley, Ocotillo Wells, Hollister Hills, Carnegie, and Clay Pit. Over $3 million has been invested in resource-management work alone. At Pismo Dunes, near San Luis Obispo, for example, by far the most popular area, barriers and fences have been installed to protect the vegetation. Without the fences, the plants would be trampled, the dunes would erode, and the area would be flattened—a dismal prospect for the one million visitors who zip over the Pismo Dunes each year.

So where does all the money come from? The California Off-Highway Division is funded entirely by user-generated fees. Gas tax from off-highway fuel supplies 75 percent, and the rest comes from savings interest, registration fees, user fees, and leases. Well-financed, well-managed, well-planned: the California Off-Highway Motor Vehicle Program is on a roll.

And so are the off-road enthusiasts. They ramble

Despite a popular state vehicular recreation area nearby, solitude isn't far away at Pismo Dunes. Two natural preserves have been established to maintain the fragile environment of dunes, beaches, and vegetation. Visitors can walk across the wind-scrolled sand to discover anything from flowers that grow nowhere else in the world to millions of monarch butterflies pausing during their annual migration. FRANK S. BALTHIS

through grassy valleys and narrow canyons at Hungry Valley off Interstate 5 at Gorman. They attend international motorcycle events at Hollister Hills, or participate in world class hill climbs at Carnegie, 14 miles east of Livermore. They take their ATVs and dune buggies down the gravel washes and over the sand dunes at Ocotillo Wells, while next door in Anza-Borrego Desert State Park, visitors watch birds, photograph spring wildflowers, and hike through canyons filled with silence. Or after tearing around Clay Pit, off-roaders are close enough to cool off in Lake Oroville.

Different people need different places. Some recreate by speeding up, others by slowing down. There's no right way or wrong way. Thanks to a Department of Parks and Recreation and to an Off-Highway Division dedicated to the maintenance of diversity, one Californian can stand in solitude and listen to a canyon wren sing, while another, a few miles away, can jump on an off-road vehicle and let the good times roll. ∎

Once a family farm that produced wild-oat hay for Wells Fargo Express teams, Hollister Hills State Vehicular Recreation Area, top, now boasts 60 miles of well-planned, well-maintained trails for a growing number of off-roaders. Strict regulations aim to minimize the numbers of accidents and injuries. CALIFORNIA DEPARTMENT OF PARKS AND RECREATION

Grafted onto the eastern edge of Anza-Borrego Desert State Park, Ocotillo Wells State Vehicular Recreation Area, bottom, is a potpourri of exciting terrain for off-roaders, including a fossil-shell reef, a sand bowl, a palm oasis, and several old military bunkers. CALIFORNIA DEPARTMENT OF PARKS AND RECREATION

New horizons

Where to from here? California is changing fast. By the year 2000 over 30 million people will live here, an increase of 7 million from 1980. And 43 percent of the total population will be composed of blacks, Asians, and Hispanics. Southern California will be predominantly Hispanic. The Asian-American population in the San Francisco Bay Area will probably double in the next decade.

A more diverse population demands a broader scope of recreation. What do immigrants from Vietnam, Poland, or Peru hope for? How can California reach out to them? A dynamic population needs a dynamic park system, one that studies the future and plans accordingly. Yet it needs a system that survives the everyday politics

and economics that grind away at the best of intentions. It needs a system that has a good offense and a good defense, that departs from tradition now and then to coevolve with a complex population. It needs a system that opens new horizons.

The California State Park System is doing just that. Two programs provide good examples. One reaches into the city, the other into the sea.

Recognizing that many inner-city residents are unable to travel to their state parks, California adopted a "bring the parks to the people" campaign in 1977 and established Candlestick Point State Recreation Area on the shoreline of San Francisco Bay just south of San Francisco. It was the state park system's first urban development. Every stitch of the planning process had strong public input. Today, when distance might make other parks inaccessible, millions of visitors can enjoy the bike trails, fishing piers, and picnic areas at Candlestick Point. People of every age, race, and income live only an hour away. The landfill on which the park is located was originally created as a navy shipyard during World War II. Today it is slowly evolving into a marshland filled with waterfowl and seabirds. Candlestick Point is just the beginning for the California State Park System. The move into the cities is more than a gesture; it's a commitment to an unwritten constitution that guarantees every Californian the right to experience his or her state parks.

Growth within a viable state park system is more than just an increase in budget and acreage.

A bat star (Patiria miniata) brightens a tide pool at Point Lobos State Reserve. Scores of invertebrates, from starfish and sea urchins to limpets and clams to crabs, await discovery in the intertidal zones on the coast of California.
KIM HEACOX

It's a matter of fine-tuning a management machine to the point of predicting problems and in best-case scenarios, of establishing new frontiers in conservation. The California State Park System has an honorable habit of doing both.

On July 1, 1960, the Point Lobos Marine Reserve became the first underwater park in the world. Like the invention of the wheel, it was an idea that made perfectly good sense and everybody wondered why nobody had thought of it before. Since then, a dozen units have been added and 50 more listed as "potentials" within the California Underwater Parks Program, formally established in 1968. Other states and countries have followed suit, from Florida to Alaska to Australia, Canada, Columbia, Japan, Mexico, and the Republic of South Africa.

The California Coast is as precious beneath the shore as it is above. In their way, the kelp forests off Point Lobos are as interesting as the redwoods. The caves and arches of Salt Point and Van Damme state parks create a maze of underwater forms. Submerged shipwrecks dot the entire coast and impart a "Long John Silver" sense of excitement and intrigue. Since sea level was much lower thousands of years ago, many underwater areas likely contain important archaeological sites. Near the La Jolla submarine canyon, for example, is a 4,000- to 5,000-year-old village submerged 80 feet. Places like this are rich with information about ancient cultures and changing landscapes.

California has nearly a half-million active, certified scuba divers, tens of thousands of whom use underwater parks each year. But don't despair, these parks aren't just for people with tanks on their backs. A growing program of intrepretive facilities—aquariums, slide shows, films, artifacts, and exhibits—will bring nondivers closer to the underwater world. In some respects, too, these parks aren't for people at all, but belong instead to the sea urchins, starfish, kelp forests, seals, sea otters, and other marine creatures that need this habitat to survive.

So who are the parks for? As Edward Abbey says, "They belong to everyone, and to no one." They are repositories of discovery and learning that teach us the greatest skill of all: how to share this earth with our fellow man and our fellow creatures. ▨

Above, diving is an increasingly popular sport in the underwater parks of the California Coast. Here a couple of divers display the large abalones they found at Año Nuevo State Reserve between Santa Cruz and Half Moon Bay. FRANK S. BALTHIS

Ice plant, right, a nonnative of California, spreads by runners and thrives on diverse terrain where other plants cannot. Here it grows on sand dunes at Bodega Head on the Sonoma Coast State Beach. WILLIAM HELSEL

Epilogue

"San Francisco was one of the richest grizzly bear habitats in North America 200 years ago," a keynote speaker tells a conference of the California State Park Ranger Association.

"The only grizzly bear in California shouldn't be on the state flag," he continues. "We need vision...vision not to think just in terms of our lifetime.

"It's not wilderness unless there's something bigger and meaner than you out there. We need to preserve a sense of danger, with grizzly bears, white-water rapids, and sea cliffs—places people can fall off of. We need that because then we aren't so arrogant."

The speaker finishes with a story about young Aldo Leopold who graduated from the Yale School of Forestry 70 years ago and went to work for the U.S. Forest Service. While in charge of a timber survey crew, he stopped to eat lunch on a hill above a stream. A she-wolf emerged from the forest to play with her pups in the water. Leopold thought there was nothing good about wolves so he and his crew emptied their rifles into the pack. He then walked down and saw a sight that permanently changed his view of wildlife.

"We reached that old wolf just in time to see a fierce green fire dying in her eyes," Leopold wrote years later.

"We've got to get that green fire back," the speaker says, "that green fire that makes the world go around. That's your job. That's our job. That's everyone's job. Rangers are the priests and priestesses of the natural world; the guardians of evolution. Don't give up. We have to keep that fierce green fire alive and put it back into California."

With the establishment of Yosemite as the first state park in 1864, and with the subsequent evolution of a million-acre state park system considered by many to be without peer, California has indeed rekindled that fire. She takes her past, present, and future seriously. The Department of Parks and Recreation sees its challenge as more than keeping that fire alive; it intends to usher California into the twenty-first century with those green flames burning even brighter than they do today. It takes great people to appreciate a great heritage; California has been blessed with both. ∎

Mule deer, left, are an important element in the balance of California's natural diversity. By feeding on acorns and the shoots of shrubs they maintain a grassland that would otherwise become wooded. Both browsers and grazers, these deer move easily from one environment to another, seeming almost to thrive at times in the face of adversity. D. CAVAGNARO

Undulating hills taper down to Morro Bay, right, where a gentle shore offers pleasant opportunities for recreation. Tremendous numbers of migrating birds rest here each spring and fall en route to lands as distant as Alaska and Argentina.
WINSTON SWIFT BOYER

California state parks directory

Sacramento/northern California parks

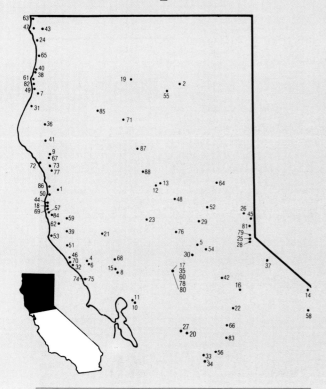

1 ADMIRAL WILLIAM STANDLEY STATE RECREATION AREA

Near the headwaters of the south fork of the Eel River, this park features some 45 acres of towering redwoods. [14 miles west of Laytonville on Branscomb Road; 45 acres, 1700' el. (707) 247-3318].

2 AHJUMAWI LAVA SPRINGS STATE PARK

Accessible only by boat, this island of old lava flows in the middle of Big Lake. Excellent hiking, fishing (trout and bass), and a view of Mount Shasta. [Rat Farm Landing, 3.5 miles north of McArthur (Highway 299 E.), 6,000 acres, 3000' el. (916) 335-2777]

3 ANDERSON MARSH

Between Lower Lake and Clear Lake on Highway 53. Historic Anderson Ranch buildings, ancient Indian sites, wetlands habitat for birdwatching. [(707) 994-0688, 279-4293]

4 ARMSTRONG REDWOODS STATE RESERVE

The outdoor Forest Theater in Armstrong seats 4,200 people. Austin Creek's open woodlands and hillsides offer a striking contrast to the adjoining primeval redwood forests of Armstrong. Look for gray foxes, bobcats, wood duck, and the 1,400-year-old Colonel Armstrong Tree. [2 miles north of Guerneville on Armstrong Woods Road; 4,900 acres, 171' el., 24 developed campsites, 4 primitive campsites. (707) 865-2391]

5 AUBURN STATE RECREATION AREA

Located on beautiful Lake Clementine, this area is perfect for individuals who enjoy sailing and swimming. Having both marina and launch areas, the park is also great for hiking and horseback riding. [1 mile south of Auburn on Highway 49; 42,000 acres, 1200' el.; 100 primitive sites. Overlook of construction site of Auburn Dam and Reservoir, where placer mining took place 1850-1920. (916) 885-4527]

6 AUSTIN CREEK STATE RECREATION AREA

See number 4. [3 miles north of Guerneville on Armstrong Woods Road, 1940' el.; 4,236 acres.]

7 AZALEA STATE RESERVE

Acres of fabulous azaleas make hiking the trails and picnicking in this reserve a real experience. [5 miles north of Arcata via U.S. 101 and North Bank Road (Highway 200); 30 acres, 150' el. (707) 677-3570 or 443-4588]

8 BALE GRIST MILL STATE HISTORIC PARK

A true part of California history, this mill was once the center of social activity as Napa Valley settlers gathered to have their corn and wheat grain ground into flour. [3 miles north of St. Helena on Highway 29/128; 1 acre, 360' el. Water-powered grist mill built in 1846. (707) 942-4575]

9 BENBOW LAKE STATE RECREATION AREA

More than 626 acres of forest and 32,000 square feet of water make Benbow a great area for hiking, fishing, swimming, and sailing. [2 miles south of Garberville on U.S. 101. 946 acres, 400' el. Closed during high water in winter. 76 developed sites; trailers 24', campers 30'. Cold showers only. (707) 247-3318]

10 BENICIA CAPITOL STATE HISTORIC PARK

Visit the restored capitol building, site of California's third seat of government (1853-54). [First and G streets, Benicia; 1 acre, 20' el. (707) 745-3385]

11 BENICIA STATE RECREATION AREA

Marshland area on Dillion's Point makes the perfect day trip for fishing fans. [1.5 miles west of Benicia via I-780; 467 acres, 0' el. Automatic gate requires entrance fee in quarters. (707) 648-1911]

12 BIDWELL MANSION STATE HISTORIC PARK

This is the Victorian, 26-room brick mansion of pioneers John and Annie Bidwell. Daily tours and special group reservations are available. [525 Esplanade, Chico; 5 acres, 195' el. Open by tour only, 10 a.m. to 5 p.m.; last tour starts at 4 p.m. (916) 459-6144]

13 BIDWELL RIVER PARK STATE RECREATION AREA

Enjoy camping, fishing, or boating. [5 miles west of Chico on River Road (off West Sacramento Avenue);180 acres, 195' el. Nature walks, tubing, canoeing. (916) 895-4303]

14 BODIE STATE HISTORIC PARK

Original, remote, unrestored, unimproved, and unvarnished, Bodie is a ghost town preserved in a state of "arrested deterioration." [13 miles east of Highway 395 on Bodie Road, 7 miles south of Bridgeport; 450 acres, 8400' el. Museum open daily during summer. Interpretive talks for groups by advance reservation. (916) 525-7232]

15 BOTHE-NAPA VALLEY STATE PARK

Stroll among the 1,242 acres of Ritchie Creek in the heart of the wine country. Hiking, with elevations that range from 400 to 2,000 feet. Look for forests of Douglas fir, tan oak, and madrone. A special feature is the Pioneer Cemetery. [4 miles north of St. Helena on Highway 29/128; 1,917 acres, 360' el. 50 developed sites; trailers 24', campers 31'. Swimming pool open mid-June through Labor Day. (707) 942-4575]

16 CALAVERAS BIG TREES STATE PARK

This park features two giant groves of redwoods, some of the oldest in California. Beaver Creek tumbles through acres of pine trees. [4 miles northwest of Arnold on Highway 4; 5,994 acres, 4700' el. 129 developed sites; trailers 27', campers 27'. Visitor center open during peak periods with herbarium, displays on nature and history. Guided hikes, campfire talks, snowshoeing, and cross-country skiing. (209) 795-2334]

17 CALIFORNIA STATE CAPITOL MUSEUM

Home of the California Legislature since 1869. Exhibits, tours 9 a.m. to 5 p.m. Capitol Mall and 10th St., Sacramento. (916) 324-0333

18 CASPAR HEADLANDS STATE BEACH/RESERVE

A hundred yards of beach adjacent to 2 acres of headlands and a panoramic ocean view, this is a good point to watch for gray whales. Fishing is good off the beach. [4 miles north of Mendocino on Highway 1, west on Point Cabrillo Drive; 3 acres, 0'-30' el. (707) 937-5804]

19 CASTLE CRAGS STATE PARK

Swim or fish in the Sacramento River, hike in the backcountry, but be sure to see the 6,000-foot glacier-polished crags for which the park is named. Offers a view of Mt. Shasta. [6 miles south of Dunsmuir on I-5; 6,218 acres, 2000' el. 64 developed sites; trailers 21', campers 27'. (916) 235-2684]

20 CASWELL MEMORIAL STATE PARK

On the banks of the Stanislaus River, good fishing—bass, catfish, sturgeon, bluegill, and in the fall, salmon and steelhead. Follow the Oak Forest Nature Trail through stands of valley oak. The great blue heron rookery is on the undeveloped west side. [6 miles south of Ripon on Austin Road; 258 acres, 40' el. 65 developed sites; trailers 31', campers 31'. (209) 599-3810]

21 CLEAR LAKE STATE PARK

This area is perfect for water activities, including fishing for largemouth bass, crappie, and channel catfish. [3.5 miles northeast of Kelseyville on Soda Bay Road; 565 acres, 1400' el. 147 developed sites; trailers 31', campers 31'. (707) 279-4293]

22 COLUMBIA STATE HISTORIC PARK

Restored gold rush town. Gold panning, stagecoach ride, exhibits, mine tours, restaurants, hotel, and stores. Interpretive slide talks. [4 miles north of Sonora via Highway 49 and county road; 273 acres, 2100' el. (209) 532-4301]

23 COLUSA-SACRAMENTO RIVER STATE RECREATION AREA

Riverbank cottonwoods and willows shelter one of the finest fishing stretches (king salmon, steelhead, rainbow trout, and striped bass) in California. The river is also on the Pacific flyway, a major migratory route for birds. [In Colusa, 9 miles east of I-5; 67 acres, 60' el. 10 developed sites, 12 primitive sites; trailers 30', campers 30'. (916) 458-4927]

24 DEL NORTE COAST/JEDEDIAH SMITH REDWOODS STATE PARKS

Located in the heart of California's rain forest bordering Oregon. Dense groves of giant redwoods grow almost to the ocean's edge, where tide pools and bluffs line the rocky Pacific shore. Black bears are occasionally seen in the backcountry, as are beavers and river otters. Catches of 30-pound steelhead are not unheard of on the Smith River, the largest undammed river in the state. [7 miles south of Crescent City on U.S. 101; 6,375 acres, 670' el. 145 developed sites; trailers 27', campers 31'. (707) 464-9533]

25 D.L. BLISS STATE PARK

One of 5 adjacent parks that include some six miles of Lake Tahoe shoreline. Hiking, swimming, and fishing. Features the Old Lighthouse and the Balancing Rock Nature Trail. [17 miles south of Tahoe City on Highway 89; 1,237 acres, 6920' el. 168 developed sites; trailers 15', campers 21'. (916) 525-7277]

26 DONNER MEMORIAL STATE PARK

The Donner Party was trapped here in the savage winter of 1846. Museum is open 10 a.m. to 4 p.m. with exhibits on the Donner Party and the area's history. [On Donner Pass Road, 2 miles west of Truckee; 353 acres, 5950' el. 154 developed sites; trailers 24', campers 28'. (916) 587-3841]

27 DURHAM FERRY STATE RECREATION AREA

A day-use park near the San Joaquin River, this area offers a large beach, with good fishing and trails that lead to the water. [Not operated by State.]

28 EMERALD BAY STATE PARK

Emerald Bay offers a panoramic view of Lake Tahoe from Eagle Falls and features Vikingsholm, a replica of a Norse fortress, open for guided tours from 10 a.m. to 4:30 p.m. between July 1 and Labor Day. [22 miles south of Tahoe City on Highway 89; 593 acres. 100 developed sites; trailers 21', campers 24'. (916) 541-3030]

29 EMPIRE MINE STATE HISTORIC PARK

Almost half of all the gold ever mined in California came from the mines of Nevada County. At the largest, the Empire Mine, you can tour the Empire Cottage and elegant gardens as well as the remaining surface structures. [10791 East Empire Street, Grass Valley; 788 acres, 2650' el. (916) 273-8522]

30 FOLSOM LAKE STATE RECREATION AREA

Set in the beautiful Sierra Nevada foothills, this 18,000-acre lake and recreation area offers hiking, camping, picnicking, horseback riding, waterskiing, boating, and swimming. [7806 Folsom-Auburn Road, Folsom; 17,718 acres, 456' el. 168 developed sites, trailers 31', campers 31'. Showers at Beals Point only. In 1895, electricity from the Folsom Powerhouse was transmitted to Sacramento, 22 miles away. Powerhouse open for groups by reservation only. (916) 988-0205]

31 FORT HUMBOLDT STATE HISTORIC PARK

This former military post, where soldiers such as Colonel Robert Buchanan and a young officer named Ulysses S. Grant kept peace in the Humbolt County region, features an historical logging display with a self-guided trail. [3431 Fort Avenue, Eureka; 12 acres, 50' el. Open during daylight hours. Group tours by appointment. (707) 443-7952]

32 FORT ROSS STATE HISTORIC PARK

This area was settled by the Russians in 1812 as an outpost for sea otter hunters and a permanent trade base. Russian Orthodox chapel and three other reconstructed Russian buildings, and a 5,000 sq. ft. visitor center with exhibits. [12 miles north of Jenner on Highway 1; 1,165 acres, 90' el. Open 10 a.m. to 4:30 p.m. (707) 865-2391]

33 FREMONT FORD STATE RECREATION AREA

Undeveloped, there is no easy access. This area offers some fishing and lots of privacy. [5 miles east of Gustine on Highway 40; 114 acres, 66' el. (209) 826-1196]

34 GEORGE J. HATFIELD STATE RECREATION AREA

Bordered on three sides by the Merced River, the park features swimming and fishing. Groves of valley oak make it a mecca for wildlife. [28 miles west of Merced on Kelly Road; 47 acres, 62' el. 7 developed sites; trailers 31', campers 32', cold showers. (209) 632-1852]

35 GOVERNOR'S MANSION

Built in 1877-78, this 15-room, five-bathroom example of Victorian-Gothic architecture became California's Executive Mansion in 1903. Since then, it has been home to 13 of our state's governors, including Earl Warren, Edmund G. "Pat" Brown, and Ronald Reagan. [16th and H streets, Sacramento; 0.25 acre, 20' el. Open by tour only from 10 a.m., last tour starts at 4:30 p.m. Tour groups limited to 25. (916) 445-4209]

36 GRIZZLY CREEK REDWOODS STATE PARK

Lying in the Van Duzen River Valley, this park has good fishing during salmon season and steelhead runs in fall and winter. Enjoy two short trails: one a self-guided nature walk, the other a walk through virgin redwood groves. [18 miles east of U.S. 101 on Highway 36; 234 acres, 375' el. 30 developed sites; trailers 24', campers 30'. Visitor center. (707) 777-3683]

37 GROVER HOT SPRINGS STATE PARK

This is true alpine beauty for the mountain lover, with one trail switchbacking up 2,000 feet of steep mountainside to Burnside Lake. Enjoy Nordic skiing and snowshoeing as well as soaking in the famous curative waters of the hot springs. [3 miles west of Markleeville on Hot Springs Road; 539 acres. 76 developed sites; trailers 24', campers 27'. Winter camping (no showers); hot springs pool open year round.]

38 HARRY A. MERLO STATE RECREATION AREA

Bordering a lagoon, this 830-acre park offers fishing and relaxation. Use of small boats is allowed. [32 miles north of Eureka on U.S. 101; 830 acres, 0' el. (707) 443-4588]

39 HENDY WOODS STATE PARK

This unique park features two virgin redwood groves: Big Hendy (80 acres) and Little Hendy (20 acres). The Navarro River runs the length of the park. [8 miles northwest of Boonville, 0.5 miles off Highway 128; 693 acres, 200' el. 92 developed sites; trailers 24', campers 30'. (707) 895-3141 or 937-5804]

40 HUMBOLDT LAGOONS STATE PARK

A seasonal lagoon situated in a wooded hillside with an extensive beach. Perfect for shore fishing and picnicking. [31 miles north of Eureka on U.S. 101; 1,490 acres, 0' el. 36 primitive sites (no water), and 6 boat-in campsites. (707) 488-2171]

41 HUMBOLDT REDWOODS STATE PARK

Home of the 33-mile Avenue of the Giants Parkway, Rockefeller Forest, and Founders Grove; dedicated to the early leaders of the Save-the-Redwoods League. Over 100 miles of hiking and riding trails, and river frontage with swimming and fishing. In the rainy season, look for runs of salmon. [45 miles south of Eureka via U.S. 101 and Highway 254 (Avenue of the Giants); 51,143 acres, 150' el. Visitor center. (707) 946-2311]

42 INDIAN GRINDING ROCK STATE HISTORIC PARK

Site of a Northern Miwok Indian "grinding rock" where acorns were ground into flour-meal. Roundhouse, dwellings, and an Indian football field. [11 miles northeast of Jackson, 1.4 miles off Highway 88 on Pine Grove-Volcano Road. 136 acres, 2418' el. 21 developed sites; trailers 24', campers 32'. No showers. Interpretive talks for groups by reservation. (209) 795-2334]

43 JEDEDIAH SMITH REDWOODS STATE PARK

See number 24. [9 miles east of Crescent City on Highway 199; 9,707 acres.]

44 JUG HANDLE STATE RESERVE

On the beautiful Mendocino Coast, enjoy a fascinating five-mile, self-guided nature trail called "The Ecological Staircase," which explores the five wave-cut terraces formed by the sea and tectonic activity. [1 mile north of Caspar on Highway 1; 769 acres, 97' el. Self-guiding nature trail (brochures sold at park) and interpretive tours; check with park for times. (707) 937-5804]

45 KINGS BEACH STATE RECREATION AREA

Ponderosa pine and small brush cover 700 feet of Lake Tahoe frontage area. This area is great for water sports in summer. [12 miles northeast of Tahoe City on Highway 28; 8 acres, 6250' el. Not operated by State.]

46 KRUSE RHODODENDRON STATE RESERVE

See number 70. Take Plantation Road, 22.5 miles north of Jenner on Highway 1. 317 acres, 500' el.

47 LAKES EARL AND TALAWA

An undeveloped area of wetlands and beautiful scenery. [8 miles north of Crescent City via U.S. 101 and Kellogg or Lower Lake Road; 4,810 acres, 10' el. (707) 443-4588]

48 LAKE OROVILLE STATE RECREATION AREA/ CLAY PIT STATE VEHICULAR RECREATION AREA

This man-made lake was formed by the tallest earth-filled dam (770 feet) in the country. Water sports are big here. See the Feather River Fish Hatchery, which was built to replace lost spawning areas for salmon and steelhead. Also, a 220-acre off-road vehicle area nearby. [7 miles east of Oroville via Highway 162; 16,100 acres land, 15,500 acres lake surface, and 157 miles of shoreline. 900' el. 212 developed campsites. Seaplane landing area. Displays on State Water Project, area's natural and cultural history at Visitor Center. (916) 533-2200]

49 LITTLE RIVER STATE BEACH

Good fishing on 10,820 feet of ocean frontage. Unpaved parking for 87 vehicles. [13 miles north of Eureka on U.S. 101; 112 acres, 0' el. (707) 677-3570 or 443-4588]

50 MacKERRICHER STATE PARK

This park has a variety of habitats: beach, bluff, headland, dune, forest, and wetland. Tidepools dot the shore; seals live in the rocks off the Mendocino Coast, and the gray whale can be seen in its annual migration. More than 90 species of birds visit or reside near Cleone Lake, a former tidal lagoon. [3 miles north of Fort Bragg on Highway 1; 1,598 acres, 50' el. 143 developed sites; trailers, 27', campers 30'. (707) 964-9112 or 937-5804]

51 MAILLIARD REDWOODS STATE RESERVE

A 600-acre grove with towering redwoods. [20 miles northwest of Cloverdale on Ornbaun Spring Road, 3.5 miles from Highway 128; 242 acres, 1000' el. (707) 937-5804]

52 MALAKOFF DIGGINS STATE HISTORICAL PARK

This was California's largest "hydraulic" mine. See the cliffs carved by the great streams of water and the 556-foot bedrock tunnel that served as a drain. [16 miles northeast of Nevada City on North Bloomfield Road. Motorhomes and trailers should use Tyler-Foote Crossing Road, 27 miles to park]; 2,700 acres, 3300' el. 30 developed sites; trailer 18', campers 24', no showers, 2 rustic cabins for rent. Interpretive talks for groups by advance reservation. Conducted tours during summer. (916) 265-2740]

53 MANCHESTER STATE BEACH

An 800-acre stretch of beach for walking, beach combing, and surf netting, with a view of Point Arena Lighthouse. Brush and Alder creeks are excellent for fishing. See coastal wildflowers: sea pinks, poppies, baby blue eyes, lupines, and wild irises. [7 miles north of Point Arena on Highway 1; 1,419 acres, 0' el. 48 primitive sites, environmental sites and group camp; trailers 22', campers 30'. (707) 937-5804]

54 MARSHALL GOLD DISCOVERY STATE HISTORIC PARK

This is the place, Sutter's Mill, where James W. Marshall found the gold nugget that changed the course of California history. Exhibits tell the story of Sutter, Marshall, and the gold rush that followed their discovery in 1848. [8 miles north of Placerville on Highway 49; 280 acres, 750' el. (916) 622-3470]

55 McARTHUR-BURNEY FALLS MEMORIAL STATE PARK

The 129-foot waterfall is the main attraction. Black swifts nest in the cliff behind the falls. Six miles of hiking trails through evergreen forests, and Lake Britton offers watersport. [11 miles northeast of Burney on Highway 89; 768 acres, 3000' el. 118 developed sites; trailers 32', campers 45'. (916) 335-2777]

56 McCONNELL STATE RECREATION AREA

A shady oasis on the banks of the Merced River where anglers can find catfish, black bass, and perch. Several grassy play areas offer kids ample room to roam. [5 miles southeast of Delhi on Pepper Road; 74 acres, 104' el. 17 developed sites; trailers 24', campers 27'. (209) 394-7755]

57 MENDOCINO HEADLANDS STATE PARK

Near quaint downtown Mendocino, this oceanfront area is great for strolling and whale watching. The Ford Museum gives weekend lectures on area wildlife. [Surrounds town of Mendocino; 347 acres, 40' el. (707) 937-5804]

58 MONO LAKE TUFA STATE RESERVE

This reserve was established to preserve the spectacular "tufa towers" of calcium carbonate. The remnant of a huge ice age lake, Mono Lake may be one million years old. It contains volcanic cinder cones and hot springs, but no fish because of its high salinity. [10 miles southeast of Lee Vining via Highways 395, 120; 17,000 acres, 6417' el. (619) 647-6331]

59 MONTGOMERY WOODS STATE RESERVE

Stroll through the 700 acres of redwoods where you can picnic and relax. [11 miles northwest of Ukiah on Comptche Road (Orr Spring Road); 1,142 acres, 1500' el. (707) 937-5804]

60 OLD SACRAMENTO STATE HISTORIC PARK/ CALIFORNIA STATE RAILROAD MUSEUM

An exciting area where shops, restaurants, offices, and museums are housed in restored or reconstructed buildings in the style of 1849-1870. The park includes the Old Eagle Theater, the B.F. Hastings Building, built in 1852-53, and the State Railroad Museum, where 21 authentically restored locomotives and cars are exhibited within its 100,000 square feet. [Front Street, Sacramento; 14 acres, 30' el. (916) 445-4209]

61 PATRICK'S POINT STATE PARK

A tree- and meadow-covered headland with high cliffs and Agate Beach, named for the semiprecious stones deposited there by the ocean. See sea lions and seals near Palmer's Point. Watch for gray whales that pass the point during the winter months. [25 miles north of Eureka on U.S. 101; 642 acres, 200' el. 8 miles of hiking trail. 123 developed sites; trailers 31', campers 31'. Museum with exhibits on natural features and Indian life. (707) 677-3570]

62 PAUL M. DIMMICK WAYSIDE CAMPGROUND

This forest of pine, oak, and redwood on the Navarro River offers fishing and canoeing during the spring. [8 miles east of Highway 1 on Highway 128; 12 acres, 45' el. 28 primitive sites; trailers 21', campers 30'. (707) 937-5804]

63 PELICAN STATE BEACH

Beautiful ocean views and offshore fishing are attractions at this five-acre undeveloped site on the Oregon border. [21 miles north of Crescent City on U.S. 101. 5 acres, 0' el. (707) 464-9533]

64 PLUMAS-EUREKA STATE PARK

The historic mining town of Johnsville and the partially restored Plumas-Eureka stamp mill recall a time when hard-rock gold mining was the primary activity in this region. Hiking, fishing, and sightseeing. [5 miles west of Blairsden on County Road A-14; 6,749 acres, 5175' el. 67 developed sites; trailers 24', campers 30'. Museum has displays on mining, pioneer life. Interpretive talks for groups by reservation. (916) 836-2380]

65 PRAIRIE CREEK REDWOODS STATE PARK

A magnificent grove of coast redwoods, with the tallest trees in the world (300 feet). Attractions include Fern Canyon Trail, where ferns cover 50-foot rock walls; Revelation Trail, with 17 informative stopping points; and Cathedral Trees Trail. [50 miles north of Eureka on U.S. 101; 12,544 acres, 150' el. Elk Prairie Campground: 5 miles north of Orick on Highway 101; 75 developed sites; trailers 24', campers 27'. Gold Bluffs Beach Campground: 3 miles north of Orick via Highway 101, Davison Road (Fern Canyon turnoff). 27 developed sites; campers 20', max., 7' wide. 70 miles of hiking trail. (707) 488-2171]

66 RAILTOWN 1897 STATE HISTORIC PARK

The Sierra Railroad's steam engines and cars here have starred in movies and television since 1919—from *High Noon* to *Little House on the Prairie*. Slide shows, a gift shop, picnic facilities, and the historic grounds are open Memorial Day through Labor Day. [5th Avenue, Jamestown; 26 acres, 2000' el. (209) 984-3953]

67 RICHARDSON GROVE STATE PARK

This cool, dark, and still forest of towering coast redwoods along the South Fork of the Eel River, is named after the state's twenty-fifth governor, Friend W. Richardson. Winter runs of silver and king salmon and steelhead trout draw many fishermen. Good hiking for all visitors. [8 miles south of Garberville on U.S. 101; 1,414 acres, 450' el. 169 developed sites; trailers 24', campers 30'. (707) 247-3318]

68 ROBERT LOUIS STEVENSON STATE PARK

In 1880 Robert Louis Stevenson spent his honeymoon here. With rough terrain, evergreen forests, and chaparral in the high ground, this park is for day use only. Hikers can climb to a scenic vista and view the entire Bay Area, Mount Shasta, and Mount Lassen—some 190 miles away. [7 miles north of Calistoga on Highway 29; 3,178 acres, 2200' el. No water or restrooms, limited parking. (707) 942-4575]

69 RUSSIAN GULCH STATE PARK

On the Mendocino Coast this redwood forest includes the Russian Gulch Creek Canyon, the Devil's Punch Bowl headland, and a beach. See the 200-foot sea-cut tunnel that collapsed at its inland end forming a "blowhole." [2 miles north of Mendocino on Highway 1; 1,300 acres, 100' el. 3-mile bicycle trail. 30 developed sites; trailers 24', campers 27'. (707) 937-5804]

70 SALT POINT STATE PARK/KRUSE RHODODENDRON STATE RESERVE

The coastline varies from sandy beach coves on the northern end to steep bluffs and sandstone cliffs at Salt Point and Gerstle Cove. Also an underwater reserve for divers. At the top of the coastal ridge is a large open "prairie" and pygmy forest. Next to Salt Point, Kruse Rhododendron State Reserve contains 317 acres of beautiful second-growth redwood, Douglas fir, tan oak, and of course, rhododendron. [20 miles north of Jenner on Highway 1; 5,970 acres, 100' el. 110 developed sites (no showers), 20 walk-in sites, 5 environmental camps, 10 camp-sites for hikers and bicyclists; trailers 31', campers 31', trailers 25', campers 25'. 10 hike-in tent sites. (707) 865-2391]

71 SHASTA STATE HISTORIC PARK

Formerly known as the lusty "Queen City" of California's northern mining district, the main feature is the 1880s Shasta County Courthouse. [6 miles west of Redding on Highway 299; 13 acres, 1000' el. Museum open 10 a.m. to 5 p.m. (916) 243-8194]

72 SINKYONE WILDERNESS STATE PARK

This park is a hike-in-only wilderness of tangled forest and rough coastline north of Fort Bragg. [30 miles west of Redway on County Road 435 (Briceland Road) or 50 miles north of Fort Bragg via Highway 1 and County Road 431 (narrow, dirt, not maintained); 5,076 acres, 0'-1800' el. No trailers or RVs. Primitive hike-in camping only; no developed water supply. (707) 247-3318]

73 SMITHE REDWOODS STATE RESERVE

Redwoods provide a pleasant wayside for passersby. [4 miles north of Leggett on U.S. 101; 622 acres, 750' el. (707) 247-3318]

74 SONOMA COAST STATE BEACH

Features 13 miles of beaches and secluded coves, rugged headlands, natural arches, tidal pools, and reefs. Five-mile system in the dunes. Great fishing. [5000 acres, 10' el. Bodega Dunes Campground 0.5 mile north of Bodega Bay on Highway 1. 98 developed sites; trailers 31', campers 31'. Wrights Beach Campground 6 miles north of Bodega Bay on Highway 1. 30 developed sites; trailers 24', campers 27'. No showers. 11 environmental campsites at Willow Creek. (707) 865-2391]

75 SONOMA STATE HISTORIC PARK

This is the site of Mission San Francisco Solano, Sonoma Barracks, Toscano Hotel, General Vallejo's home. [Spain Street at 3rd Street West, Sonoma: first home of General Vallejo. Spain Street at 1st Street East: Sonoma Mission, most northerly Franciscan mission, contains Jorgensen Collection of mission paintings; Toscano Hotel; Sonoma Barracks, Mexican garrison, and scene of 1846 Bear Flag Revolt. Open 10 a.m. to 5 p.m. No fires. 64 acres, 90' el. (707) 938-1578; school res. 938-1519]

76 SOUTH YUBA TRAIL

Eight miles northwest of Nevada City on Highway 49 this park has 2 miles of trails accessible to people in wheelchairs. (916) 273-3884.

77 STANDISH-HICKEY STATE RECREATION AREA

The south fork of the Eel River winds through second-growth redwoods, and steep trails line the river canyon. Steelhead and salmon spawn in the fall and winter. A scenic feature is the Captain Miles Standish tree, a 225-foot redwood, 40 feet in circumference, with an estimated age of 1,200 years. [1 mile north of Leggett on U.S. 101; 1,020 acres, 800' el. 162 developed sites; trailers 24', campers 27'. (707) 925-6482]

78 STATE INDIAN MUSEUM

On the grounds of Sutter's Fort, Native American structures have been built in an outdoor demonstration area. [2612 K Street, Sacramento. 20' el. Open 10 a.m. to 5 p.m. (916) 445-4209]

79 SUGAR PINE POINT STATE PARK

Along the basin of General Creek, this forest is one of the finest remaining natural areas on Lake Tahoe. Deep-line anglers fish the lake's 300-foot-deep underwater ledges for trout and salmon. See Ehrman Mansion, a stunning summer home built in 1903. [10 miles south of Tahoe City on Highway 89; 2,011 acres, 6250' el., 175 developed sites; trailers 24', campers 30'. Year-round camping. The Ehrman Mansion is open from noon until 4 p.m. during the summer. Cross-country ski trail. (916) 525-7982]

80 SUTTER'S FORT STATE HISTORIC PARK

This is Sacramento's earliest European-style settlement, restored to its 1846 appearance. John Sutter established his fort in 1839. [2701 L Street, Sacramento; 6 acres, 20' el. Open 10 a.m. to 5 p.m. Entrance fee includes self-guided tour. (916) 445-4209]

81 TAHOE STATE RECREATION AREA

Located in the middle of Tahoe City. A lake view and groves

of Ponderosa and Jeffery pine. Enjoy watersports. [0.25 mile east of Tahoe City on Highway 28; 57 acres, 6250' el. 39 developed sites; trailers 15', campers 21'. (916) 583-3074]

82 TRINIDAD STATE BEACH

Adjacent to Patrick's Point, with hiking trails and picnic facilities, this is an off-the-beaten-path kind of place. [19 miles north of Eureka on U.S. 101; 159 acres, 50' el. (707) 677-3570 or 443-4588]

83 TURLOCK LAKE STATE RECREATION AREA

This park is ideal for water-oriented recreation. Bound on the north by the Tuolumne River and on the south by Turlock Lake. Fish for black bass, crappie, bluegill, and catfish. For day use, there are two large picnic areas and two swimming beaches. [22 miles east of Modesto off Highway 132; 408 acres, 248' el. 65 developed sites; trailers 24', campers 27'. (209) 874-2056]

84 VAN DAMME STATE PARK

This park has 1,831 acres of beach and upland on the Mendocino Coast, featuring the Fern Canyon scenic trails system; the Pygmy Forest and the Cabbage Patch, where skunk cabbage grows abundantly. [3-mile south of Mendocino on Highway 1; 2,163 acres, 15' el. 74 developed sites, 10 environmental campsites; trailers 27', campers 30'. 3 miles bicycle trail. (707) 937-0851 or 937-5804]

85 WEAVERVILLE JOSS HOUSE STATE HISTORIC PARK

"The Temple of the Forest beneath the Clouds" is the oldest continuously used Chinese temple in California. See the Chinese art objects, pictures, mining tools, and weapons used in the 1854 Tong War. [50 miles west of Redding on Highway 299; 3 acres, 2000' el. Open for tours 10 a.m. to 5 p.m. (916) 623-5284]

86 WESTPORT-UNION LANDING STATE BEACH

On the Mendocino Coast with two miles of beach, this park is ideal for ocean fishing and picnicking. [1.5 miles north of Westport on Highway 1; 41 acres. Primitive campsites. (707) 937-5804]

87 WILLIAM B. IDE ADOBE STATE HISTORIC PARK

Home of the president of the short-lived Bear Flag Republic, this park features a restored smokehouse, carriage shed, and a genuine covered wagon. [2 miles northeast of Red Bluff on Adobe Road; 3 acres, 275' el. Open 8 a.m. to 5 p.m. (916) 527-5927]

88 WOODSON BRIDGE STATE RECREATION AREA

Nestled in oak woods on the Sacramento River, fishing and bird-watching is superb here. [6 miles east of Corning and I-5 on South Avenue; 428 acres, 200' el. 46 developed sites; trailers 31', campers 31'. (916) 839-2112]

Park facilities and features

#	Park	Family Campsites	Environmental Campsites	Family & Sites for Hikers & Bicyclists	Picnicking	Enroute Campsites	Hiking Trail	Fishing	Swimming	Boating	Horseback Riding Trails	Exhibits	Nature Trail	Food Services	Supplies	Trailer Sanitation Station	Designated Underwater Area
1	Admiral William Standley State Recreation Area																
2	Ahjumawi Lava Springs State Park		•		•												
3	Anderson Marsh				•		•	•					•				
4	Armstrong Redwoods State Reserve			★	•							•	•				
5	Auburn State Recreation Area	•	•		•		•	•	•								
6	Austin Creek State Recreation Area	•			•			•									
7	Azalea State Reserve				•								•				
8	Bale Grist Mill State Historic Park											★					
9	Benbow Lake State Recreation Area				•	★	•	•	•	•	★						
10	Benicia Capitol State Historic Park											•					
11	Benicia State Recreation Area				•			•									
12	Bidwell Mansion State Historic Park											★					
13	Bidwell River Park SRA	•	•		•			•		•							
14	Bodie State Historic Park											•					
15	Bothe-Napa Valley State Park			★	★		★		★			•	★			•	
16	Calaveras Big Trees State Park	★	•		★		•	•	•			★	★			•	
17	California State Capitol Museum											★	★	★			
18	Caspar Headlands State Beach/Reserve							•									
19	Castle Crags State Park	•	•		•		•	★	•				•				
20	Caswell Memorial State Park	•	•		•		•	•				★	•				
21	Clear Lake State Park			★	★		•	★	•	★			•			•	
22	Columbia State Historic Park				★							★	•	★	★		
23	Colusa-Sacramento River State Recreation Area	★			★		•	•		•			•			•	
24	Del Norte Coast/Jedediah Smith Redwoods State Parks			★	•		•	•				•	•			•	
25	D.L. Bliss State Park	•			•		•	•	•				•				
26	Donner Memorial State Park	•			★		•	•	•			★	•				
27	Durham Ferry State Recreation Area*																
28	Emerald Bay State Park	•			•		•	•	•			•					
29	Empire Mine State Historic Park				★		•					•	★				
30	Folsom Lake State Recreation Area		•	★	★		•	★	•	★			•	★		•	
31	Fort Humboldt Historic Park				★							★					
32	Fort Ross State Historic Park				•		★	•				★					•
33	Fremont Ford State Recreation Area							•									
34	George J. Hatfield State Recreation Area	•			•			•	•								
35	Governor's Mansion											•					
36	Grizzly Creek Redwoods State Park	★			★		•	•				★	★				
37	Grover Hot Springs State Park	•			•			•	•	★							
38	Harry A. Merlo State Recreation Area							•	•								
39	Hendy Woods State Park	★			★		★	•	•				•			•	
40	Humboldt Lagoons State Park	•	•		•	•	•	•					•				
41	Humboldt Redwoods State Park		•	★	★		•	•	•	•		★	★				
42	Indian Grinding Rock State Historic Park	•	•		•							•	•				
43	Jedediah Smith Redwoods State Parks			•	•		•	•				★	★			•	
44	Jug Handle State Reserve				•								•				

Park facilities and features

#	Park	Family campsites	Environmental campsites	Family & sites for hikers & bicyclists	Picnicking	Enroute campsites	Hiking trail	Fishing	Swimming	Boating	Horseback riding trails	Exhibits	Nature trail	Food services	Supplies	Trailer sanitation station	Designated underwater area
45	Kings Beach State Recreation Area				•			•	•	•							
46	Kruse Rhododendron State Reserve						•				•		•				
47	Lakes Earl and Talawa		•		•		•	•	•								
48	Lake Oroville State Recreation Area	★	•		★	•	•	•	•	★	★	•	★	•		•	•
49	Little River State Beach							•									
50	MacKerricher State Park		★	★			★	•				•				•	•
51	Mailliard Redwoods State Reserve				•												
52	Malakoff Diggins State Historical Park	★	•		★		•		★			•	★		•		
53	Manchester State Beach		•	•	•			•								•	•
54	Marshall Gold Discovery State Historic Park				★		•	•				★	★				
55	McArthur-Burney Falls Memorial State Park	★	•		★		•	★	★	★		★	★	★	★	•	
56	McConnell State Recreation Area	•			•			•	•								
57	Mendocino Headlands State Park							•	•								
58	Mono Lake Tufa State Reserve							•					•				
59	Montgomery Woods State Reserve				•								•				
60	Old Sacramento State Historic Park/CA State Railroad Museum											★		★	★		
61	Patrick's Point State Park		★	★			★	•				★	•				
62	Paul M. Dimmick Wayside Campground	•			•			•	•								
63	Pelican State Beach							•									
64	Plumas-Eureka State Park	★			★		•	•	★			★	•				
65	Prairie Creek Redwoods State Park		•	•	•		★	•				★	★				
66	Railtown 1897 State Historic Park				•							★					
67	Richardson Grove State Park		★	★	•		•	•				•	★	★			
68	Robert Louis Stevenson State Park				•		•						•	•			
69	Russian Gulch State Park		★		•		•	•									•
70	Salt Point State Park/Kruse Rhododendron State Reserve		•	•	★		★	•								•	•
71	Shasta State Historic Park				•							•					
72	Sinkyone Wilderness State Park		•	•	•		•										
73	Smithe Redwoods State Reserve				•			•	•								
74	Sonoma Coast State Beach		•	★	★	•	★	•				•	★			•	•
75	Sonoma State Historic Park				•		★						★				
76	South Yuba Trail						★										
77	Standish-Hickey State Recreation Area		★	★			•	•	•								
78	State Indian Museum											★					
79	Sugar Pine Point State Park	•			★		★	★	•			•	★			•	
80	Sutter's Fort State Historic Park											★					
81	Tahoe State Recreation Area	•			•			•	•	•							
82	Trinidad State Beach						•	•									
83	Turlock Lake State Recreation Area	•			•		•	•	•	•	★			★	★		
84	Van Damme State Park		•	•	•	•	•	•					•				•
85	Weaverville Joss House State Historic Park													•			
86	Westport-Union Landing State Beach	★				★		•									
87	William B. Ide Adobe State Historic Park				★			•						•			
88	Woodson Bridge State Recreation Area	★						•	•				•				

* Not operated by State of California
• Features available
★ Features available and accessible to the physically disabled

Volunteers appreciated: State Park Cooperating Associations

Be nice to the person behind the counter in the gift shop at the visitor center. Chances are he or she is a volunteer, one of the 13,000 who help to run the 82 nonprofit California State Park Cooperating Associations.

These associations operate the publication and gift sales areas inside many state parks and visitor centers. Profits from the sales of interpretive items are used to build museums and visitor centers, purchase equipment for slide shows, operate rides, establish research libraries, build bridges, run campgrounds, and much more. Trained volunteers, or docents, donated over 374,000 hours of their own time in 1985 to provide thousands of interpretive walks and talks for the visiting public.

If you are interested in becoming a state park volunteer and working to make an even better California State Park System, contact a ranger in your nearest park or write to: California Department of Parks and Recreation, Office of Public Relations, P.O. Box 942896, Sacramento, CA 94296-0001.

San Francisco Bay Area parks

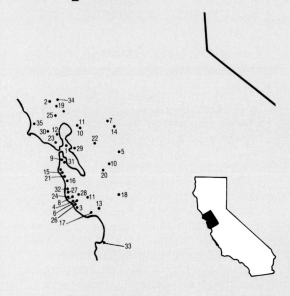

1 ANGEL ISLAND STATE PARK

First discovered in 1775 by Juan Manuel de Ayala, this mountainous, forest-covered island in San Francisco Bay offers spectacular views of Marin County, San Francisco, and the Golden Gate. A special feature is the "Cove to Crest" Natural Trail, a two-mile loop that explores the terrain of the island which has been used as an immigrant quarantine station, Nike missile base, military overseas staging area. [By ferry from Tiburon or San Francisco; 790 acres, 10′ el. Environmental campsites by reservation only, mooring facilities. (415) 435-1915]

2 ANNADEL STATE PARK

Rolling hills, woodlands, grassy meadows strewn with wildflowers (buttercups, poppies, mule ears), lush canyons full of ferns, redwoods, and Douglas fir cover this 5,000-acre park. Lake Ilsanjo offers black bass and scrappy bluegill. Ledson Marsh features 130 species of birds such as Cooper's hawks, great blue herons, and even the pileated woodpecker. [Channel Drive east of Montgomery Drive, Santa Rosa; 4,913 acres, 300′ el. No fires. (707) 539-3911]

3 AÑO NUEVO STATE RESERVE

In addition to magnificent vistas of shoreline, coastal lowlands, and the Santa Cruz Mountains are the park's most striking inhabitants—a large colony of northern elephant seals. Male seals (called bulls) 14 to 16 feet long are found here. Look for them in the December-March breeding season. [27 miles south of Half Moon Bay on Highway 1; 1,192 acres. 0′ el. (415) 879-0227]

4 BEAN HOLLOW STATE BEACH

One of the nine San Mateo County state beaches where fishing, picnicking, and beach-combing are the major activities; the cold water, rip currents, and heavy surf make swimming dangerous. Of special interest are the numerous tidepools with their fragile marine environments. Look for anemones, crabs, and sea urchins. [17.5 miles south of Half Moon Bay on Highway 1; 44 acres, 0′ el. (415) 726-6238]

5 BETHANY RESERVOIR STATE RECREATION AREA

A lovely place for water-oriented activities, this area features a bike trail and many windmills. [7 miles north of Highway 580 via Altamont Pass, Mountain House, Kelso, and Christensen roads; 300 acres, 247′ el. Northern terminus of California Aqueduct bike trail. (415) 687-1800]

6 BIG BASIN REDWOODS STATE PARK

This is the oldest park in the California State Park System, acquired in 1902. It features more than 40 miles of hiking trails with a number of beautiful waterfalls, a wide variety of environments, plenty of animals, and lots of bird life. The stars of the park are, of course, the stately redwood groves. [20 miles north of Santa Cruz via Highways 9, 236; 15,647 acres, 1000′ el. 143 developed sites; trailers 27′, campers 31′. 45 developed walk-in sites. Reserve campsites for hikers and bicyclists with park. (408) 338-6132]

7 BRANNAN ISLAND/FRANK'S TRACT STATE RECREATION AREAS

Located in the Sacramento-San Joaquin Delta, this 40-by-25-mile tangle of rivers, sloughs, levees, marshes, and old river channels snakes in all directions. One of the outstanding water-oriented recreation areas in the world, this area offers great fishing—striped bass, sturgeon, catfish, bluegill, perch, and bullhead. Little Frank's Tract, a protected wetland marsh, is home to beaver, muskrat, river otter, mink, and 76 species of birds. [3 miles south of Rio Vista on Highway 160; 336 acres, 25′ el. 102 developed sites; trailers 31′, campers 31′. Swimming beach open all year. Lifeguards on duty from mid-June through Labor Day. By boat, 8 miles southeast of Rio Vista; 3,515 acres, 11′ el. (916) 777-6671]

8 BUTANO STATE PARK

This 2,200-acre redwood park in the Santa Cruz Mountains, has plenty of good hiking. During the summer, park rangers lead guided nature walks and weekend campfire activities.

[7 miles south of Pescadero on Cloverdale Road; 2,186 acres, 500′ el. 21 developed sites; trailers 24′, campers 30′; 19 developed walk-in sites. (415) 879-0173]

9 CANDLESTICK POINT STATE RECREATION AREA

This area offers a beautiful view of San Francisco Bay with picnic areas, fishing, and hiking trails. [East of U.S. 101 via Candlestick exit (adjacent to south and east sides of stadium), San Francisco; 37 acres, 0′ el. (415) 557-4069]

10 CARNEGIE STATE VEHICULAR RECREATION AREA

A 1,500-acre haven for off-road motorcyclists; four-wheel-drive vehicles are allowed, too, but only by the creek bed. [14 miles east of Livermore on Telsa/Corral Hollow Road; 1,540 acres, 600′-3000′ el. 100 miles of trails for motorcycles only; groups should make reservations with park. (415) 447-9027]

11 CASTLE ROCK STATE PARK

There are beautiful vistas in this 3,200-foot altitude park with oak and pine forests and many springs and waterfalls. [2 miles south of intersection of Highways 9 and 35 on Skyline Blvd.; 3,025 acres, 3215′ el. 25 primitive walk-in sites. (408) 867-2952]

12 CHINA CAMP STATE PARK

With 1,500 acres of natural watershed along the shores of San Francisco Bay, extensive intertidal, salt marsh, meadow, and oak habitats are home to a variety of wildlife. The key attraction is the historic remains of China Camp, once a thriving fishing village. [North of San Rafael via U.S. 101 and North San Pedro Road; 1,512 acres, 0′ el. 30 walk-in campsites. (415) 456-0766]

13 FOREST OF NISENE MARKS STATE PARK

This park offers 10,000 acres of rugged semiwilderness, rising from sea level to steep coastal mountains of more than 2,600 feet. Fifteen miles of trails lead from cool redwood forests to the warmer upper ridges. Evidence of logging operations, mill sites, and trestles can still be found along the way. [4 miles north of Aptos on Aptos Creek Road; 9,960 acres, 800′ el. Reserve hike-in camp with park. (408) 335-5858]

14 FRANK'S TRACT STATE RECREATION AREA

See number 7.

15 GRAY WHALE COVE STATE BEACH

One of nine San Mateo County state beaches, this is excellent for viewing the gray whale migration. [Not operated by State. 9 miles north of Half Moon Bay on Highway 1; 0.3 acre, 0′ el.]

16 HALF MOON BAY STATE BEACH

Another of the nine San Mateo County state beaches, it features a trail for horseback riding that runs behind the beach parallel to the spectacular ocean frontage. [0.5 mile west of Highway 1 on Kelly Avenue, Half Moon Bay; 170 acres. 51 developed sites;

trailers 36', campers 36'. Cold outdoor showers. (415) 726-6238]

17 HENRY COWELL REDWOODS STATE PARK

Fifteen miles of hiking and riding trails loop through a forest that looks much the same today as it did 200 years ago when Zayante Indians found shelter, water, and game here. This is the home of Redwood Grove, with its self-guided nature path. You can also find Douglas fir, madrone, oak, and the most unusual feature of the park, a stand of Ponderosa pine. [5 miles north of Santa Cruz on Highway 9; campground 3 miles east of Felton on Graham Hill Road; 4,082 acres, 500' el. 113 developed sites; trailers 24', campers 31'. (408) 335-4598]

18 HENRY W. COE STATE PARK

There are some 32,000 acres of solitude in this expanse of rough, undeveloped park. Nature trails, horseback riding, and a small museum on early California ranching are other features. [14 miles east of Morgan Hill on East Dunne Avenue; 32,230 acres, 2200' el. 20 primitive sites; trailers 18', campers 26'. 21 backpacking sites. Pine Ridge Museum, interpreting ranch life in the late 1880s, open 9 a.m. to 4 p.m. Saturdays and Sundays only. (408) 779-2728]

19 JACK LONDON STATE HISTORIC PARK

Once part of the famous writer's 1,500-acre Beauty Ranch, the site features the ruins of Wolf House, the custom-built dream home that burned in 1913 before he moved in, London's grave site, and the House of Happy Walls, built by the writer's wife after his death. [1.5 miles west of Glen Ellen on London Ranch Road. 759 acres, 650' el. Self-guided history trail. Hours 8 a.m. to sunset, museum open 10 a.m. to 5 p.m. No fires. (707) 938-5216; school res. 938-1519]

20 LAKE DEL VALLE STATE RECREATION AREA

This 4,000-acre park and 750 acres of lake is ideal for picnicking, horseback riding, boating, fishing, and swimming. A special feature is the lake tour boat. [Not operated by State.]

21 MONTARA STATE BEACH

One of the nine San Mateo County state beaches, Montara is quickly becoming one of the more popular sun and surf areas. Explore the tidepools or fish the ocean. A dormitory-style hostel on the grounds of Montara Point Lighthouse is operated by American Youth Hostel Association. [8 miles north of Half Moon Bay on Highway 1; 55 acres, 0' el. (415) 726-6238, hostel—728-7177]

22 MOUNT DIABLO STATE PARK

Experts say that the view from the summit of Mount Diablo is unsurpassed except by Mt. Kilimanjaro. If you have binoculars you can even pick out Half Dome in Yosemite Park. Lots of good hiking and rock climbing available, too. [5 miles east of Highway 680, Danville, on Diablo Road; 14,688 acres, 3849' el. 60 developed sites; trailers 19', campers 31'. No showers. (415) 837-2525]

23 MOUNT TAMALPAIS STATE PARK

In beautiful Marin County, just north of the Golden Gate, the view from the summit is awe-inspiring. The shining spires of San Francisco can be seen to the south, the bay and Mount Diablo to the east, the blue Pacific to the west. Some 30 miles of trails and Mountain Theater, a natural amphitheater on the eastern slope, are other featured attractions. [6 miles west of Mill Valley on Panoramic Highway; 6,205 acres, 2586' el. 16 developed walk-in sites, group camp. No showers. (415) 388-2070]

24 PESCADERO STATE BEACH

This is another one of the nine San Mateo County state beaches. The tidepools here offer excellent viewing of delicate marine life. There is also a marshy 210-acre wildlife refuge, the home of blue herons, kites, deer, raccoons, foxes, and skunks. [14.5 miles south of Half Moon Bay on Highway 1; 638 acres, 0' el. (415) 726-6238]

25 PETALUMA ADOBE STATE HISTORIC PARK

Main residence of Rancho Petaluma, the 66,000-acre agricultural empire that made General Mariano Guadalupe Vallejo one of the wealthiest and most powerful men in the Mexican Province of California, 1834-1846. Authentic furniture and exhibits depict early ranch life. [0.7 mile east of Petaluma on Highway 116, 2 miles north on Casa Grande Road; 41 acres, 150' el. Open 10 a.m. to 5 p.m. (707) 762-4871]

26 PIGEON POINT LIGHTHOUSE

Guided tours are available. Hostel on grounds operated by American Youth Hostel Association. [Not operated by State. 0.25 mile west of Highway 1 on Pigeon Point Road, approximately 30 miles north of Santa Cruz. (415) 879-0633 after 4:30 p.m.]

27 POMPONIO STATE BEACH

One of the nine San Mateo County state beaches offering swimming and sunbathing. [12 miles south of Half Moon Bay on Highway 1; 410 acres, 0' el. (415) 726-6238]

28 PORTOLA STATE PARK

This park offers a rugged, natural basin forested with coast redwoods, Douglas fir, and live oak. Ten miles of trails crisscross the deep canyon and its two streams, Peters Creek and Pescadero Creek. Sharp eyes will spot clam shells and other marine deposits, indicating the ocean that once covered the area. [Portola Spring Road, 6.5 miles west of Highway 35 on Alpine/State Park Road; 2,010 acres, 450' el. 52 developed sites; trailers 21', campers 27'. Reserve hike-in campsites with park. (415) 948-9098]

29 ROBERT W. CROWN MEMORIAL STATE BEACH

Located across the Bay from San Francisco, this beach is a good park with extensive facilities for day use—playground, fishing, swimming, volleyball, and sailing. Features include an estuary/reserve and programs on beach wildlife at the visitor center. [Not operated by State.]

30 SAMUEL P. TAYLOR STATE PARK

This area features approximately 2,700 acres of beautifully wooded countryside in the steep, rolling hills of Marin County. Cool, shaded, fern-filled groves of coast redwoods contrast with dry, open grassland where oak, tan oak, madrone, and other hardwoods are dominant. [15 miles west of San Rafael on Sir Francis Drake Blvd.; 2,800 acres, 150' el. 68 developed sites; trailers 18', campers 24'. 2 group sites; 1 horse camp; 12.7 miles of hiking trail. (415) 488-9897]

31 SAN BRUNO MOUNTAIN STATE PARK

Operated by San Mateo County, this mountain area has complete day-use facilities. (415) 992-6770 or 363-4020

32 SAN GREGORIO STATE BEACH

One of the nine San Mateo County state beaches offering swimming and sunbathing. [10.5 miles south of Half Moon Bay on Highway 1; 172 acres, 0' el. (415) 726-6238]

33 SOUTH MONTEREY BAY DUNES

[Sand Dunes Drive at Highway 1; 26 acre, 0' el. (408) 649-2836]

34 SUGARLOAF RIDGE STATE PARK

Here the headwaters of Sonoma Creek run through gorge and canyon then across the meadow floor beneath scenic rock outcroppings. Some 25 miles of trails offer hiking and horseback riding through the chaparral, forests, and serpentine rock of the Mayacamas Range. Look for deer, raccoons, and gray foxes. [7 miles east of Santa Rosa on Highway 12, north on Adobe Canyon Road (3 miles); 2,373 acres, 1100'el. 50 primitive sites; trailers 22', campers 22'. (707) 833-5712]

35 TOMALES BAY STATE PARK

This is a recreation haven on the Point Reyes peninsula. The shallow, gently sloping, surf-free beaches have good populations of horseneck clams and cockles. Inland, the park is a lush wilderness of forests, fields, hills, meadows, and swamps. Some 30 varieties of wildflowers attract botanists and flower lovers. One of the finest groves of Bishop pine in California is preserved in the Jepson Memorial Grove. [4 miles north of Inverness on Sir Francis Drake Blvd.; 2,038 acres, 86' el. Camping area for bicyclists. (415) 699-1140]

Making reservations

You need reservations to camp overnight in a state park, especially during the busy summer months. You can reserve a campsite in your favorite park up to eight weeks in advance by calling MISTIX at 1-800-952-5580 (in California) or (916) 452-1950 for out-of-state reservations. The TTY number for the hearing impaired is (916) 324-1891. The nightly reservation fee, which you can charge to Visa or Mastercard, varies depending on the facilities available and the location of the campsite. A coastal park campsite with hookups for a motor home, for example, is the most expensive, and a primitive campsite (pit toilets, no showers) is the least. There is a nonrefundable service charge for booking the reservation, and if you change your plans, you will be subject to an alteration fee.

Reservations for Hearst Castle tours are also available at the telephone numbers listed above. Although you may make tour reservations upon your arrival at Hearst Castle, avoid any last-minute disappointment or inconvenience by making them in advance.

The *Guide to California State Parks* contains information on every park unit, including campgrounds, facilities, and telephone numbers for each one. The guide is available at your nearest park, or by mail for $2 from California Department of Parks and Recreation, Publications Office, P.O. Box 942896, Sacramento, CA 94296-0001.

Park facilities and features

#	Park	Family Campsites	Environmental Campsites	Family & Sites for Hikers & Bicyclists	Picnicking	Enroute Campsites	Hiking Trail	Fishing	Swimming	Boating	Horseback Riding Trails	Exhibits	Nature Trail	Food Services	Supplies	Trailer Sanitation Station	Designated Underwater Area
1	Angel Island State Park		★		★		•	★		★		★	•	★			
2	Annadel State Park				•		•	•			•						
3	Año Nuevo State Reserve				•		•	•					•	★			
4	Bean Hollow State Beach				•			•					•				
5	Bethany Reservoir State Recreation Area				★			★		★							
6	Big Basin Redwoods State Park		★	•		★					•	★	★	★	★	•	
7	Brannan Island/Frank's Tract State Recreation Areas		★	★			★	•	★			★		★		•	
8	Butano State Park		•	•		•											
9	Candlestick Point State Recreation Area				★		★	★									
10	Carnegie State Vehicular Recreation Area	•			•									•			
11	Castle Rock State Park	•			•		•					•					
12	China Camp State Park	•			★		•	★		•	•	★		★			
13	Forest of Nisene Marks State Park	•			•		•										
14	Frank's Tract State Recreation Area							•	•	•							
15	Gray Whale Cove State Beach							•									
16	Half Moon Bay State Beach		★	•	•		•					•				•	
17	Henry Cowell Redwoods State Park		★	★		•	•				•	★	★	★		•	
18	Henry W. Coe State Park		•	•		•					•	•	•				
19	Jack London State Historic Park				★		★										
20	Lake Del Valle State Recreation Area*																
21	Montara State Beach						•			•							
22	Mount Diablo State Park	★	•		★		★					•	•				
23	Mount Tamalpais State Park	•	•		★	•	★	•				•	•	•	★		
24	Pescadero State Beach							•									
25	Petaluma Adobe State Historic Park				•							•					
26	Pigeon Point Lighthouse*																
27	Pomponio State Beach				•			•									
28	Portola State Park	•			•		•					•	•				
29	Robert W. Crown Memorial State Beach*																
30	Samuel P. Taylor State Park	★	★	★	★		•	•			•	★	•				
31	San Bruno Mountain State Park *																
32	San Gregorio State Beach				•			•					•				
33	South Monterey Bay Dunes							•									
34	Sugarloaf Ridge State Park	•			•		•					•	•	•			
35	Tomales Bay State Park				★		•	•	•			★	•				

* Not operated by State of California
● Features available
★ Features available and accessible to the physically disabled

Central California parks

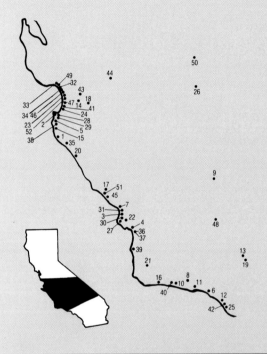

1 ANDREW MOLERA STATE PARK

A Big Sur-area state park, this one is still relatively undeveloped. It offers great hiking opportunities as well as fishing and beachcombing. [21 miles south of Carmel on Highway 1; 4,786 acres, 60' el. Primitive walk-in campsites. (408) 667-2315]

2 ASILOMAR STATE BEACH & CONFERENCE GROUNDS

The name means "a refuge by the sea," and that it is. The Asilomar Conference Center can hold groups of 15 to 850. With 103 acres of pine forest, the grounds offer breathtaking view of cypress, surf, and sand. [Asilomar Avenue, Pacific Grove; 105 acres, 0' el. (408) 372-8016]

3 ATASCADERO STATE BEACH

Good surf fishing and swimming at this beach. [Highway 1 at Yerba Buena, Morro Bay; 75 acres, 0' el. 104 developed sites; trailers 24', campers 24'. Outdoor cold showers. (805) 772-2560]

4 AVILA STATE BEACH

A relatively small beach, there is still good fishing from the pier. [Operated by San Luis Obispo County.]

5 CARMEL RIVER STATE BEACH

A Monterey Bay state beach. A "must-see" is the bird sanctuary at the lagoon, which plays host to a wide variety of waterfowl and songbirds. [From Highway 1 in Carmel via Ocean Avenue and Scenic Road; 106 acres, 0' el. (408) 624-4909]

6 CARPINTERIA STATE BEACH

Seals, sea lions (December through May), and an occasional gray whale can be seen from 4,100 feet of ocean frontage. Also look for tidepools—starfish, sea anemones, crabs, snails, octopi, and sea urchins. [12 miles south of Santa Barbara on U.S. 101, 50 acres, 0' el. 174 developed sites; trailers 30', campers 30', 86 sites with electricity, water, and sewer hookups. (805) 684-1855]

7 CAYUCOS STATE BEACH

This is a very small beach, good for day use. [Operated by San Luis Obispo County.]

8 CHUMASH PAINTED CAVE STATE HISTORIC PARK

This sandstone cave houses religious drawings of the Chumash Indians, as well as likenesses of coastal fishermen that date back into the 1600s. [3 miles south of San Marcos Pass, Highway 154, on Painted Caves Road; 7 acres, 1750' el. (805) 968-0019]

9 COLONEL ALLENSWORTH STATE HISTORIC PARK

Allensworth was founded in 1908 by Colonel Allen Allensworth and four others as a self-governed town for blacks. Start your tour with a 30-minute film at the visitor center, then visit the restored school and envision a time when black pioneers, people of vision and courage, first settled the town. [20 miles north of Wasco on Highway 43, 15 miles west of Earlimart on County Road J22; 240 acres, 205' el. Exhibit trailer; group tours by reservation. (805) 849-3433]

10 EL CAPITAN STATE BEACH

Exactly 9,450 feet of well-developed beach, including overnight camping facilities, fishing, and picnic areas with 3.5 miles of bike trails. [20 miles northwest of Santa Barbara on U.S. 101; 133 acres, 0' el. 140 developed sites; trailers 27', campers 30'. (805) 968-1411]

11 EL PRESIDIO DE SANTA BARBARA STATE HISTORIC PARK

This is the site of the oldest building in Santa Barbara and the second-oldest in California, El Cuartel. Step back and view this historical site, all that remains of the four Spanish-Mexican Era presidios, amid the modern buildings. [210 East Canon Perdido, Santa Barbara. 2 acres, 75' el. Open Monday through Friday, 10 a.m. to 5 p.m. (805) 966-9719]

12 EMMA WOOD STATE BEACH

Moderate ocean temperatures make for great swimming and surfing. Perch, bass, cabezon, and corbina make for excellent fishing. A freshwater marsh at the southwest end attracts raccoons, various songbirds, and red-tailed hawks. [4 miles north of Ventura on U.S. 101; 116 acres, 0' el. 150 primitive sites; trailers 31', campers 31'. Only group camp is operated by State. (805) 654-4611]

13 FORT TEJON STATE HISTORIC PARK

Established by the U.S. Army in 1854, this post is one of the significant remaining links to the early American occupation period. [40 miles south of Bakersfield, 90 miles north of Los Angeles on I-5; 205 acres, 3250' el. Museum exhibits on army life, local history. Group tours by appointment. Mock Civil War skirmish held by volunteers on third Sundays of summer months. (805) 248-6447]

14 FREMONT PEAK STATE PARK

Grasslands in the peaks of the Gabilan Range feature hiking trails with expansive views of Monterey Bay. [11 miles south of San Juan Bautista on San Juan Canyon Road; 244 acres, 2750' el. 25 primitive sites; trailers 18', campers 26'. (408) 623-4255]

15 GARRAPATA STATE BEACH

This beach offers two miles of newly developed beachfront, with coastal hiking and a 50-foot climb to a beautiful view of the blue Pacific. It also features outstanding coastal headlands at Sobranes Point. [On Highway 1, 6.7 miles south of Rio Road, Carmel (18 miles north of Big Sur); 2,800 acres, 50' el. (408) 667-2315]

16 GAVIOTA STATE PARK

Opportunities for fishing, surfing, swimming, sailing, or sunbathing can be found here. Nearby campsites offer shade under the existing salt cedar trees. [33 miles west of Santa Barbara on U.S. 101; 2,776 acres, 0' el. 59 developed sites; trailers 25', campers 27'. (805) 968-0019]

17 HEARST SAN SIMEON STATE HISTORICAL MONUMENT

Once you tour the esplanade and gardens, the three guest houses, the theater, the Gothic, Doges, and Celestial suites, the 5,000-book library, the displays of Renaissance art in the Della Robbia Room, the indoor Roman pool, the "New Wing" (three floors of guest suites with Persian rugs and paintings by the Old Masters), the wine cellar and vaults...you'll understand why the castle took 28 years to complete. [At town of San Simeon; 149 acres, 1600' el. Open 8 a.m. to 3:20 p.m. daily (except Thanksgiving, Christmas, and New Year's Day) by tour only. (805) 927-4621]

18 HOLLISTER HILLS STATE VEHICULAR RECREATION AREA

With two ranches in the Gabilan Mountains and elevations from 660 to 2,425 feet, this is an off-road vehicle paradise. The Upper Ranch has a fenced motocross track and can be reserved for special events. The Lower Ranch, set aside for motorcycle and ATC use only, has eight miles of trails and several hill climbs. [8 miles south of Hollister via Cienega Road; 3,322 acres, 800' el. 100 primitive sites; trailers 18', campers 26'. 100 miles of trails for motorcycles only; 4-wheel-drive group day use or camping by reservation. (805) 927-4621]

19 HUNGRY VALLEY STATE VEHICULAR RECREATION AREA

This area offers a variety of terrains for motorcycle and 4-wheel-drive enthusiasts—more than 15,000 acres available for trail riding. For a change of pace hike into the preserve, where a seep provides water for valley oak and native grasses. [From I-5 at Gorman, 1 mile north on Peace Valley Road; entrance is at USFS campground; 19,000 acres, 4000' el. Off-highway vehicle use. Primitive camping, no water. (805) 248-6447]

20 JULIA PFEIFFER BURNS STATE PARK

This park stretches from the legendary Big Sur coastline into nearby 3,000-foot ridges. Features include redwood, tan oak, madrone, chaparral, and an 80-foot waterfall that drops from granite cliffs right into the ocean. A unique feature: a 1,680-acre underwater reserve protecting a spectacular assortment of marine life. Look for seals, sea lions, and playful sea otters in the cove. [37 miles south of Carmel on Highway 1; 3,543 acres, 400'el. (408) 667-2315]

21 LA PURÍSIMA MISSION STATE HISTORIC PARK

This is the most completely restored of California's 21 Spanish missions. Start at the visitor center with historical information, displays, and artifacts. Then follow the self-guided tour through church, shops, quarters, springhouse, the cemetery, and the mission gardens for a step back into the primitive pastoral California of the early 1800s. [3 miles northeast of Lompoc on Purisima Road; 967 acres, 75' el. Open 9 a.m. to 5 p.m., guided tours by appointment. (805) 733-3713]

22 LOS OSOS OAKS STATE RESERVE

This reserve is a walking loop through an undeveloped preserve of oak groves. [8 miles northwest of U.S. 101 on Los Osos Valley Road, 2 miles south of San Luis Obispo; 85 acres, 0' el. (805) 772-2560]

23 MANRESA STATE BEACH

A Monterey Bay state beach, a favorite activity here is digging for the Pismo clam. Light fishing and surfing are other attractions. [13 miles south of Santa Cruz on Highway 1, take San Andres Road; 83 acres, 0' el. Lifeguard in summer. (402) 724-1266 or 688-3241]

24 MARINA STATE BEACH

This day-use beach is known for its hang-gliding activities. Also sunbathing and picnic areas are popular attractions. [Foot of Reservation Road in Marina. 10 miles north of Monterey; 131 acres, 0' el. (408) 649-2836]

25 McGRATH STATE BEACH

This area is ideal for camping by the beach. Plenty of water sports available or simply relax in the sun. [From U.S. 101, Ventura, take Seaward Avenue then south on Harbor; 295 acres, 0' el. 174 developed sites; trailers 30', campers 34'. (805) 654-4611]

26 MILLERTON LAKE STATE RECREATION AREA

The lake, formed by the Friant Dam across the San Joaquin River, has 43 miles of shoreline for water sports. The surrounding hills offer good hiking, and a surprising variety of wildlife can be observed— ground squirrels, cottontails, mule deer, badgers, and bald and golden eagles. The park also contains the original Millerton County Courthouse, built in 1867. [Park headquarters 20 miles northeast of Fresno via Highway 41 and Friant Road; campground on north shore 20 miles east of Madera via Highway 145 and North Fork Road; 6,553 acres, 600' el. 131 developed sites; trailers 30', campers 31'. Outdoor cold showers. (209) 822-2225 or 822-2332]

27 MONTAÑA DE ORO STATE PARK

Features here include rugged cliffs, secluded sandy beaches, coastal plains, streams in wooded canyons, grass- and chaparral-covered hills, and 1,347-foot Valencia Peak. The park gets its name, "Mountain of Gold," from a profusion of wildflowers in spring. At dusk, black-tailed deer browse on the coastal plain. Also, look for the black oystercatcher with its crimson bill. [7 miles south of Los Osos on Pecho Road; 7,328 acres, 50' el. 50 primitive sites; trailers 24', campers 24'. (805) 772-2560]

28 MONTEREY STATE BEACH

This is a favorite place for surfers and tidepool watchers. Good fishing, too. [Del Monte Avenue and Camino Aguajito, Monterey; 14 acres, 0' el. (408) 649-2836]

29 MONTEREY STATE HISTORIC PARK

Here the U.S. flag was first officially raised on July 7, 1846, bringing 600,000 square miles, including California, into the Union. Ten buildings—including the Custom House (built in 1827), California's first theater (1846-47), and several former residences, now museums, built in the 1830s preserve the rich heritage of early California. [210 Olivier Street, Monterey; 7 acres, 0' el. House museums open 9 a.m. to 5 p.m. Guided tours of Larkin House, Casa Soberanes, Stevenson House. (408) 649-2836]

30 MORRO BAY STATE PARK

This central coast area features a museum of natural history, a lagoon, and natural bay habitat. There is also an abundance of sailing, fishing, and hiking. Be sure to view all the exhibits at the museum. [In Morro Bay; 2,035 acres, 0' el. 115 developed sites; trailers 31', campers 31'. 20 sites with electricity and water hookups for 31 foot vehicles. (805) 772-2560]

31 MORRO STRAND STATE BEACH

A coastal frontage park and a getaway to experience the view and make use of the picnic sites available. [2 miles south of Cayucos on Highway 1; 34 acres, 0' el. (805) 772-2560]

32 MOSS LANDING STATE BEACH

A Monterey Bay state beach where you can experience offshore fishing and utilize the horseback riding trails. [In Moss Landing take Jetty Road from Highway 1; 55 acres, 0' el. (408) 688-3241]

33 NATURAL BRIDGES STATE BEACH

Another Monterey Bay state beach. Photographers, artists, and sightseers appreciate the picturesque arches cut by ocean waves in a sandstone out-cropping for which the beach is named. The annual migration of monarch butterflies is another featured attraction here. Eucalyptus is the butterflies' main source of food, and they cluster in the tree's branches in cold weather. [On West Cliff Drive, Santa Cruz; 65 acres, 0' el. (408) 423-4609 or 688-3241]

34 NEW BRIGHTON STATE BEACH

Still another Monterey Bay state beach with picnic areas, swimming, fishing, and a nearby forest of Monterey pine. [4 miles south of Santa Cruz on Highway 1; 94 acres, 0' el. 115 developed sites including 15 walk-in; trailers 31', campers 31'. (408) 475-4850 or 688-3241]

35 PFEIFFER BIG SUR STATE PARK/BIG SUR

River flats and canyons, cut by the Big Sur River, are home to coast redwoods, sycamores, cottonwoods, maples, alders, and willows. Wild boars are common, as are raccoons, skunks, and, along the creek, birds such as water ouzels and belted kingfishers. Hike on the many scenic trails, including a self-guided nature loop near the lodge and exhibit shelter. [26 miles south of Carmel on Highway 1; 821 acres, 215' el. Motel-type cabins for rent. 217 developed sites; trailers 24', campers 27'. (408) 667-2315]

36 PISMO DUNES STATE VEHICULAR RECREATION AREA

There are 2,500 acres of sand dunes in this off-highway vehicle area where dune buggies and other specialized vehicles may operate. [3 miles south of City of Pismo Beach on beach; 500 campers permitted on sand, no designated sites. Chemical toilets. 2,500 acres, 0' el. (805) 541-1163]

37 PISMO STATE BEACH

The beach offers multiple attractions: swimming and fishing, of course; digging of the famous Pismo clams; the annual winter migration of millions of monarch butterflies; and the special, fragile environment of the dunes themselves. [2 miles south of City of Pismo Beach on Highway 1. 2,065 acres, 10' el. 143 developed sites; trailers 31', campers 36'. 42 sites with electricity, water and hookups for 31-foot vehicles. (805) 489-8655]

38 POINT LOBOS STATE RESERVE

A famous artist once called this "the greatest meeting between land and water in the world." The landscape is a mosaic of bold headlands, irregular coves, and rolling meadows. Also,

750 offshore acres form one of the richest underwater habitats in the world. A diver's paradise. Look for seals, sea lions, sea otters, and the migrating gray whales, which spout and dive offshore from December to May. [3 miles south of Carmel on Highway 1; 1,325 acres. (408) 624-4909]

39 POINT SAL STATE BEACH

This is a small, undeveloped beach. [Contact La Purísima Mission State Historical Park. (805) 733-3713]

40 REFUGIO STATE BEACH

One of the more complete beaches near Santa Barbara with superb coastal fishing. Enjoy walking one of the many trails or relax at one of the picnic sites. [23 miles northwest of Santa Barbara on U.S. 101; 155 acres, 0' el. 85 developed sites; trailers 27', campers 30'. (805) 963-1350]

41 SALINAS RIVER STATE BEACH

Many species of birds live at or visit this as well as other Monterey Bay state beaches. Look for Western meadowlarks, hawks, jays, valley quail, finches, towhees, and sparrows as well as shorebirds that winter along the bay. [1 mile south of Moss Landing, take Potrero from Highway 1; 246 acres, 0' el. (408) 688-3241]

42 SAN BUENAVENTURA STATE BEACH

This day-use-only beach features a bicycle trail and a parcours exercise trail. [From U.S. 101 in Ventura, take Seaward Avenue; 114 acres, 0' el. (805) 654-4611]

43 SAN JUAN BAUTISTA STATE HISTORIC PARK

This is the site of one of California's 21 Franciscan missions, founded in 1797. The mission church, the largest of its kind in California, has been in continuous use since July 1, 1812. Other structures built in the 1800s include several houses, the Plaza hotel and stable, a blacksmith shop, granary, and the jail. [In city of San Juan Bautista; 6 acres, 210' el. Open 10 a.m. to 4:30 p.m. (408) 623-4881]

44 SAN LUIS RESERVOIR STATE RECREATION AREA

Nestled in the grassy hills near historic Pacheco Pass, this park includes O'Neill Forebay and the Los Banos Reservoir. Outstanding fishing—bass, catfish, crappie, and bluegill, from late February through the summer. Also a good place to look for golden eagles, migratory geese, and 10 species of ducks. [12 miles west of Los Banos on Highway 152; 26,026 acres, 400' el. 79 developed sites, 34 primitive sites; trailers 27', campers 37'. Motorbike trail. (209) 826-1196]

45 SAN SIMEON STATE BEACH

This site gives campers the opportunity to hike, swim, fish, or sunbathe. [5 miles south of San Simeon on Highway 1; 541 acres, 0' el. 115 primitive sites; trailers 31', campers 31'. (805) 927-4621]

46 SEACLIFF STATE BEACH

A Monterey Bay state beach favored for the fishing pier and concrete ship. A good location for swimming. [5.5 miles south of Santa Cruz on Highway 1; 85 acres, 0' el. 26 sites with electricity, water, sewer hookups; trailers 31', campers 31'. Interpretive Center open in summer or for groups by reservation. (408) 688-3222 or 688-3241]

47 SUNSET STATE BEACH

A Monterey Bay state beach. A favorite spot for seekers of the Pismo clam. Clam diggers should beware, however, of heavy surf, riptides, and the uneven bottom. [16 miles south of Santa Cruz via Highway 1 and San Andreas Road; 324 acres, 0' el. 90 developed sites; trailers 31', campers 31'. (408) 724-1266 or 688-3241]

48 TULE ELK STATE RESERVE

Tule elk, once numerous in California, are now greatly reduced in number and all have come from a single herd at the reserve. Best viewing is around 2 p.m. during the summer. Picnic areas and interpretive exhibits. [3 miles west of I-5, off Stockdale Highway; 946 acres, 300' el. Interpretive talks for groups by appointment. (805) 765-5004]

49 TWIN LAKES STATE BEACH

The beach offers ocean swimming with lifeguards on duty. [At Santa Cruz Small Craft Harbor; 110 acres, 0' el. Snack bar, lifeguards in summer. (408) 688-3241]

50 WASSAMA ROUND HOUSE STATE HISTORICAL PARK

[55 miles north of Fresno via Highways 41, 49; 9.9 acres, 2300' el. (209) 822-2332]

51 WILLIAM RANDOLPH HEARST MEMORIAL STATE BEACH

The beach offers a little relaxation after a visit to the mansion of the late media baron. Daily tours, restaurants and hotels nearby. (See number 17.) At town of San Simeon on Highway 1. 8 acres, 0' el. (805) 927-4621]

52 ZMUDOWSKI STATE BEACH

As with other Monterey Bay state beaches, this is a popular fishing spot—perch, kingfish, sole, flounder, halibut, bocaccio (tomcod), jacksmelt, lingcod, cabezon, salmon, steelhead, and occasional rockfish. [1 mile north of Moss Landing on Highway 1, take Struve Road; 177 acres, 0' el. (408) 688-3241]

Park facilities and features

		FAMILY CAMPSITES	ENVIRONMENTAL CAMPSITES	FAMILY & SITES FOR HIKERS & BICYCLISTS	PICNICKING	ENROUTE CAMPSITES	HIKING TRAIL	FISHING	SWIMMING	BOATING	HORSEBACK RIDING TRAILS	EXHIBITS	NATURE TRAIL	FOOD SERVICES	SUPPLIES	TRAILER SANITATION STATION	DESIGNATED UNDERWATER AREA
1	Andrew Molera State Park				•			•	•		•						
2	Asilomar State Beach and Conference Grounds				•				•								
3	Atascadero State Beach	•						•	•								
4	Avila State Beach*																
5	Carmel River State Beach							•									
6	Carpinteria State Beach		★	★				•	•						★	•	
7	Cayucos State Beach*																
8	Chumash Painted Cave State Historic Park											•					
9	Colonel Allensworth State Historic Park	•			★							★					
10	El Capitan State Beach		★	★	•	•	•	•	•				•	★	★	•	
11	El Presidio de Santa Barbara State Historic Park																
12	Emma Wood State Beach				•			•	•								
13	Fort Tejon State Historic Park				★							★					
14	Fremont Peak State Park	•	•			•		•									
15	Garrapata State Beach							•	•								
16	Gaviota State Park		★			•	★	•	•	•				★	★		
17	Hearst San Simeon State Historical Monument											★	•	★			
18	Hollister Hills State Vehicular Recreation Area	•											•	•			
19	Hungry Valley State Vehicular Recreation Area	•															
20	Julia Pfeiffer Burns State Park			★	•												•

#	Park	Family Campsites	Environmental Campsites	Family & Sites for Hikers & Bicyclists	Picnicking	Enroute Campsites	Hiking Trail	Fishing	Swimming	Boating	Horseback Riding Trails	Exhibits	Nature Trail	Food Services	Supplies	Trailer Sanitation Station	Designated Underwater Area
21	La Purísima Mission State Historic Park			★		★					●	★					
22	Los Osos Oaks State Reserve												●				
23	Manresa State Beach							●					●				
24	Marina State Beach							●									
25	McGrath State Beach			★				●	●							●	
26	Millerton Lake State Recreation Area	●		★			★	★	★	●	●	●				●	
27	Montaña De Oro State Park	●	●		●		●	●			●		●				
28	Monterey State Beach								●								
29	Monterey State Historic Park											●					
30	Morro Bay State Park	★		★	●	●		●	●	●		★	●	★		●	
31	Morro Strand State Beach				●			●	●								
32	Moss Landing State Beach							●		●							
33	Natural Bridges State Beach				★			●					●				
34	New Brighton State Beach			★	★	●		●	●							●	
35	Pfeiffer Big Sur State Park/Big Sur			★	●			●			●	●	★	★	●		
36	Pismo Dunes State Vehicular Recreation Area	●			●		●	●	●	●							
37	Pismo State Beach				●	●		●	●				●			●	
38	Point Lobos State Reserve				★		★						●				●
39	Point Sal State Beach							★									
40	Refugio State Beach			★	★	●	●	●	●					★	★		
41	Salinas River State Beach							●		●							
42	San Buenaventura State Beach				★			●	●				●				
43	San Juan Bautista State Historic Park				★							★					
44	San Luis Reservoir State Recreation Area	★			★			★	★	★		★					
45	San Simeon State Beach			●	●			●								●	
46	Seacliff State Beach	★			●	●		★	●			●		★			
47	Sunset State Beach			★	★	●		●						●			
48	Tule Elk State Reserve				★							★					
49	Twin Lakes State Beach							●	●					★			
50	Wassama Round House State Historic Park				●												
51	William Randolph Hearst Memorial State Beach				●			★	●	●							
52	Zmudowski State Beach							●		●							

* Not operated by State of California
● Features available
★ Features available and accessible to the physically disabled

California Department of Parks and Recreation: Its goals and objectives

The California Department of Parks and Recreation has direct responsibility to acquire, protect, develop, and interpret for the inspiration, use, and enjoyment of the people of California, the outstanding scenic, recreational, and historical areas of the state. Since 1926 more than 285 units have been added to the state park system.

The Department of Parks and Recreation, with the assistance of the California State Park and Recreation Commission, determines the primary significance and use of acquired lands and classifies them as state parks, beaches, historic monuments, historic parks, state vehicular recreation areas, reserves, or wilderness areas.

Each year more than 64 million visitors take advantage of the recreational opportunities made available in the California State Park System. The California Department of Parks and Recreation strives to meet the changing needs of the state's dynamic and growing population, while holding in trust for future generations the irreplaceable portions of California's natural and historic heritage.

Los Angeles area parks

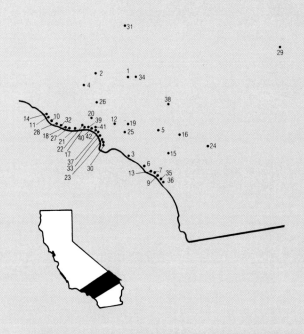

1 ANTELOPE VALLEY CALIFORNIA POPPY RESERVE

Some 1,700 acres have been reserved for viewing California's official flower—the poppy. Take a walk on one of the many trails or stop in the solar-heated museum. [15 miles west of Lancaster on Avenue I;. 1,745 acres, 2800' el. Spring wildflower area. (805) 724-1180 or 942-0662]

2 ANTELOPE VALLEY INDIAN MUSEUM

Open every second Saturday of the month, this historical museum explores the cultures of the Indian tribes that once inhabited California. [15 miles east of Lancaster on Avenue M between 150th and 170th streets east. Call for hours, information. (805) 942-0662]

3 BOLSA CHICA STATE BEACH

A popular summer night activity here is barehanded fishing for California grunion, a species that only spawns on sandy southern California beaches. With a fishing license you can catch the wiggling fish between June 1 and March 31 of the following year—a real challenge. So is surf fishing for perch,

corbina, croaker, cabezon, and sand shark. [3 miles west (upcoast) of Huntington Beach on Highway 1; 164 acres, 0' el. Fire rings, dressing rooms, cold showers, bicycle trail, paved ramp for beach wheelchair access. (714) 848-1566]

4 CASTAIC LAKE STATE RECREATION AREA

This area is a reservoir of the state water project. With 29 miles of shoreline, the lake is a major boating, fishing, and swimming attraction for southern Californians. A featured attraction is the 425-foot-tall Castaic Dam. [Operated by Los Angeles County.]

5 CHINO HILLS STATE PARK

[Take Ramona-Rincon Road off Highway 71 just north of Corona; 7,000 acres, 1000' el. (213) 620-3342]

6 CORONA DEL MAR STATE BEACH

Operated by the city of Newport, this sandy beach is approximately 0.5 mile long with excellent swimming opportunities.

7 CRYSTAL COVE STATE BEACH

With 3.5 miles of beach and 2,000 acres of undeveloped woodland, this area is excellent for hiking and horseback riding. [Between Corona del Mar and Laguna Beach on Highway 1; 1,850 acres, 0' el. 3 miles of beach; lifeguard only in season. Open daylight hours. (714) 848-1566]

8 DOCKWEILER STATE BEACH

Some three miles long, this beach offers a picnic area and concession stand. [Operated by Los Angeles County.]

9 DOHENY STATE BEACH

Actually this is two parks in one—the southern area is for camping, and the northern area for day use. The latter area features a five-acre lawn surrounded by extensive picnic facilities. Surfing is popular, but restricted to the north end of the beach. [South end of Dana Point on Highway 1; 62 acres, 0' el. 118 developed sites; trailers 24', campers 28'. (714) 496-6171]

10 EL MATADOR STATE BEACH

This small beach has a rocky shoreline and intimate coves. [10 miles west (upcoast) of Malibu on Highway 1; 18 acres, 0' el. (213) 706-1310]

11 EL PESCADOR STATE BEACH

Another small beach on 10 acres of land; picnicking and swimming are featured activities. [10 miles west (upcoast) of Malibu on Highway 1; 10 acres, 0' el. (213) 706-1310]

12 EL PUEBLO DE LOS ANGELES STATE HISTORIC PARK

See the first American building in Los Angeles. Browse through the surrounding stores and dine in the restaurants featured in a quaint setting. [Operated by the City of Los Angeles.]

13 HUNTINGTON STATE BEACH

This is one of the five Orange Coast area state beaches and a nesting sanctuary for the California least tern, a rare and endangered bird species . Breeding pairs arrive in May and can be seen from a distance at the south end of the beach. [Highway 1 at Highway 39; 78 acres, 0' el. Fire rings, cold showers, bicycle trail, paved ramp for beach wheelchair access. (714) 536-3053]

14 LA PIEDRA STATE BEACH

Two miles of fairly undeveloped beach with picnic facilities. Sunbathing and swimming are favored. [10 miles west (upcoast) of Malibu on Highway 1; 9 acres, 0' el. (818) 706-1310]

15 LAKE ELSINORE STATE RECREATION AREA

With 40 acres of grassland and lake frontage, this recreational area offers swimming, fishing and boating opportunities. Contact nature by walking one of the many trails. [22 miles southeast of Corona via Highway 71 and 74; 2,954 acres, 1234' el. 176 developed sites; trailers 28', campers 31'. 132 of the sites have electric hookups. (714) 674-3177]

16 LAKE PERRIS STATE RECREATION AREA

Formed by Perris Dam, the lake offers water sports and a special scuba diving area. Ducks and Canada geese abound, as do rainbow trout, catfish, and Alabama spotted bass. Also, thousands of acres of rugged surrounding land are open to hiking and in a special area just south of the dam, rock climbing. [11 miles southeast of Riverside (use Highway 60 or Highway 215); 8,000 acres, 1575' el. 167 developed sites, 264 sites with electricity, water, and sink water disposal hookups; trailers 27', campers 27'. (714) 657-0676]

17 LAS TUNAS STATE BEACH

This small 1,300-foot beach is operated by Los Angeles County.

18 LEO CARRILLO STATE BEACH

Famous for its 6,600-foot beach and more than 1,000 acres of upland, where elevations reach 1,500 feet, there is lots of good hiking, but watch for the plentiful poison oak. [28 miles west of Santa Monica on Highway 1; 1,602 acres, 0' el. 138 developed sites; trailers 31', campers 31'. 50 sites near beach accessible only to vehicles less than 8' in height. (818) 706-1310]

19 LOS ANGELES STATE AND COUNTY ARBORETUM

The main attraction here is the Lucky Ballroom. Beautiful plants, trees, and flowers of all species are also featured. [Operated by Los Angeles County.]

20 LOS ENCINOS STATE HISTORIC PARK

This was the center of an early California rancho. Tour the original nine-room de la Osa Adobe, the two-story limestone Garnier House, the Reyes Hut, the springs, and the lake (shaped like a Spanish guitar). [16756 Moorpark Street, Encino; 5 acres, 757' el. Exhibits on early California ranch life. Open 1 to 5 p.m., Wednesday through Sunday. (818) 706-1310]

21 MALIBU CREEK STATE PARK

More than 4,000 acres of mountain park where hiking, fishing, camping, bird watching, and horseback riding are the main features. [4 miles south of U.S. 101 on Las Virgenes/Malibu Canyon Road, Calabasas; 5,000 acres, 700' el. (818) 706-1310]

22 MALIBU LAGOON STATE BEACH

This is a famous old surf riding beach with a fishing pier. Stop at the visitor center and tour historic buildings, including Adamson House. [Upcoast of Malibu Pier where Pacific Coast Highway (Highway 1) crosses Malibu Creek; 76 acres, 0' el. (818) 706-1310]

23 MANHATTAN STATE BEACH

This is a day beach with picnic facilities. Great for sunbathing and swimming. [Operated by Los Angeles County.]

24 MOUNT SAN JACINTO STATE PARK/STATE WILDERNESS

This is a true high-country wilderness area with granite peaks, forests, and fern-bordered mountain meadows. Look for bighorn sheep on the steep eastern slopes. A popular attraction is the breathtaking Palm Springs Aerial Tramway, a 2.5-mile ride that rises almost 6,000 feet into the park from Chino Canyon near Palm Springs. [On Highway 243 near Idyllwild; 13,522 acres, 5500'-10804' el. 33 developed sites, 50 primitive sites; trailers 24', campers 24'. Wilderness hike-in camping; permits required. (714) 659-2607]

25 PIO PICO STATE HISTORIC PARK

The 13-room U-shaped mansion is the former residence of Pio Pico, the last governor of Mexican California before the American takeover in 1846. [6003 Pioneer Blvd., Whittier; 3 acres, 50' el. Open 10 a.m. to 5 p.m. Wednesday through Sunday. (714) 848-1566]

26 PLACERITA CANYON STATE PARK

Operated by Los Angeles County, this wilderness area, once dominated by gold miners, has excellent group camping and picnic facilities.

27 POINT DUME STATE BEACH

At the north end of Malibu, this is more than two miles of beach for day use only. [Operated by Los Angeles County.]

28 POINT MUGU STATE PARK

This park features five miles of beautiful ocean shoreline with rocky bluffs, sandy beaches, a spectacular sand dune, rugged hills and uplands, two major river canyons, and wide grassy valleys which are dotted with sycamores, oaks, and a few native walnuts. There are more than 70 miles of hiking trails and good swimming, body surfing, beachcombing, and surf fishing. [15 miles south of Oxnard on Highway 1; 14,980 acres, 0' el. 50 developed sites, 100 primitive sites; trailers 31',

campers 31'. Trails may be used by bicycles. (818) 706-1310 or (805) 987-3303]

29 PROVIDENCE MOUNTAINS STATE RECREATION AREA

This park is located in a sun-scorched land of broad valleys, cactus, creosote bush, sand dunes, cinder cones, and dramatic pinyon-clad mountain ranges in the eastern Mojave Desert. Special features include Mitchell Caverns National Preserve, where El Pakiva and Tecopa caverns, filled with intricate limestone formations, are open to the public. [17 miles northwest of Highway 40 near Essex on Essex Road; 5,250 acres, 4300' el. 6 primitive sites; trailers 31', campers 32'. Mitchell Caverns open by tour only; daily at 1:30 p.m. in winter. Weekends only in summer. No phone.]

30 REDONDO STATE BEACH

Good for fishing and picnicking, this beach is rough for swimming. Day use only. [Operated by Los Angeles County.]

31 RED ROCK CANYON STATE PARK

With its scenic desert cliffs, buttes, and spectacular rock formations, this park was made for camera buffs. Each tributary canyon is unique, with colors ranging dramatically from stark white to vivid reds and dark chocolate browns. After a wet winter the floral displays are stunning. Look for roadrunners, hawks, lizards, mice, and squirrels. [25 miles northeast of Mojave on Highway 14; 3,984 acres, 2600' el. 50 primitive sites; trailers 30', campers 30'. (805) 942-0662]

32 ROBERT H. MEYER MEMORIAL STATE BEACH

Three small contiguous beaches, El Matador, El Pescador, and La Piedra, run up the coast 10 miles from Malibu. See numbers 10,11, and 14, respectively. (818) 706-1310

33 ROYAL PALMS STATE BEACH

This beach is good for fishing and picnicking, but rough for swimming. Day use only. [Operated by Los Angeles County.]

34 SADDLEBACK BUTTE STATE PARK

This park was originally established in the Mojave Desert in 1960 to preserve its Joshua tree woodland. To the east rises 3,651-foot Saddleback Butte. A key attraction is the self-guided Joshua Trail. [17 miles east of Lancaster on Avenue J East; 2,875 acres, 2700' el. 50 primitive sites; trailers 30', campers 30'. (805) 942-0662]

35 SAN CLEMENTE STATE BEACH

Surfing is big on the north end of the one-mile beach. Other popular activities are skin diving for abalone and spiny lobster and walking on the trails along the bluffs. [South end of San Clemente on Highway 5; 110 acres, 100' el. 85 developed sites. Trailers 24', campers 28'. 72 sites with electricity, water, and sewer hookups for 30-foot vehicles. (714) 492-3156]

36 SAN ONOFRE STATE BEACH

This beach offers a great place for a walk, either along the 3.5 miles of sandy beaches or through the six access trails cut into the towering bluffs. The beach area is undeveloped, and plans call for it to remain in its primitive, unspoiled condition. [3 miles south of San Clemente on Highway 5 (Basilone Road); 3,036 acres, 100' el. 221 developed sites, outside cold showers; trailers 30', campers 30'. 20 primitive walk-in sites. (714) 492-4872]

37 SANTA MONICA STATE BEACH

Although geared for day use only, there are a picnic area, shops, and pier. Activities include volleyball, basketball, and running along the beach. [Operated by Los Angeles County.]

38 SILVERWOOD LAKE STATE RECREATION AREA

Formed by 249-foot Cedar Springs Dam, the lake features trout, largemouth bass, catfish, and bluegill planted by the California State Department of Fish and Game. Plenty of picnic areas, including three that can be reached only by boat. Look for Canada geese. An occasional bald eagle fishes the lake in winter. [30 miles north of San Bernardino on Highway 138; 2,200 acres, 3400' el. 136 developed sites; trailers 31'. campers 34'. Bicycle trail. (619) 389-2281 or 389-2303]

39 TOPANGA STATE BEACH

This beach is located at the foot of Topanga State Park in the Santa Monica Mountains. [Operated by Los Angeles County.]

40 TOPANGA STATE PARK

This park is in the tan cliffs and canyons of the Santa Monica Mountains. A popular attraction is the Trippet Ranch self-guided nature trail, which begins at a pond, passes through open grassland, runs by a dense canopy of live oaks, and finally opens onto chaparral-covered slopes overlooking the ocean. [From Highway 101 in Woodland Hills, south on Topanga Canyon Road, 7 miles to Entrada Road. Turn west to park. Trail camps only (1 mile hike/ride) with water, toilets, hitching rails, water troughs. For hikers, bicyclists, equestrians. 9,181 acres, 1500' el. (818) 706-1310]

41 WILL ROGERS STATE BEACH

[Operated by Los Angeles County.]

42 WILL ROGERS STATE HISTORIC PARK

This is the ranch of the famous humorist who became the most beloved man of his generation. Included are hiking trails and an audio tour of the grounds as well as a tour of Will Rogers' home. (213) 454-8212

Park facilities and features

#	Park	Family Campsites	Environmental Campsites	Family & Sites for Hikers & Bicyclists	Picnicking	Enroute Campsites	Hiking Trail	Fishing	Swimming	Boating	Horseback Riding	Trails	Exhibits	Nature Trail	Food Services	Supplies	Trailer Sanitation Station	Designated Underwater Area
1	Antelope Valley California Poppy Reserve				•								★					
2	Antelope Valley Indian Museum												★	•				
3	Bolsa Chica State Beach			★	•			★	•					★				
4	Castaic Lake State Recreation Area				•													
5	Chino Hills State Park				•													
6	Corona Del Mar State Beach*																	
7	Crystal Cove State Beach							•	•	•								•
8	Dockweiler State Beach*																	
9	Doheny State Beach			★	★			•	•				★		★	•	•	•
10	El Matador State Beach				•				•									
11	El Pescador State Beach				•				•									
12	El Pueblo De Los Angeles State Historic Park*																	
13	Huntington State Beach				•			★	★						★			
14	La Piedra State Beach				•				•									
15	Lake Elsinore State Recreation Area	★			★			•	•	•				•				
16	Lake Perris State Recreation Area	★			★		★	★	•	•	•	•	★		★		•	•
17	Las Tunas State Beach*																	
18	Leo Carrillo State Beach			★				•	•							•	•	
19	Los Angeles State and County Arboretum*																	
20	Los Encinos State Historic Park				★								★					
21	Malibu Creek State Park				★		•	•			•	•			•			
22	Malibu Lagoon State Beach				•			•	•				★	★				
23	Manhattan State Beach*																	
24	Mount San Jacinto State Park/State Wilderness		•	•	•		•											
25	Pio Pico State Historic Park				★								★					
26	Placerita Canyon State Park*																	
27	Point Dume State Beach*																	
28	Point Mugu State Park			★	★		★	•	•		•	★				•		
29	Providence Mountains State Recreation Area	•											•	•				
30	Redondo State Beach*																	
31	Red Rock Canyon State Park	★			•		•				•	•			•			
32	Robert H. Meyer Memorial State Beach				•				•									
33	Royal Palms State Beach*																	
34	Saddleback Butte State Park	★			•		•						★	•		•		
35	San Clemente State Beach			★	•			•	•	•					'	'		
36	San Onofre State Beach			★			•	•	•	•						•		
37	Santa Monica State Beach*																	
38	Silverwood Lake State Recreation Area			★	★		★	★	★	★		★	•	★	★	•		
39	Topanga State Beach*																	
40	Topanga State Park	•			•		•				•	•						
41	Will Rogers State Beach*																	
42	Will Rogers State Historic Park				★			•			•	•						

* Not operated by State of California
● Features available
★ Features available and accessible to the physically disabled

California State Parks Foundation

The California State Parks Foundation was formed in 1969 in an effort by private citizens to strengthen the state park system and to preserve California's rich natural and cultural heritage. Since its inception, the foundation has completed 53 projects and raised over $60 million.

The foundation accepts gifts and grants from private individuals, foundations, and corporations and serves as a conduit for the acquisition of lands for state parks and for the development of resources within the state park system. Currently the foundation is working with state park advisory, volunteer, and cooperating association groups on over 22 projects throughout California.

Private individuals may become foundtion members and enjoy a wide range of benefits such as boating passes, travel services, and discounts on admissions to state park concerts and performances. For more information on how you can help build a stronger and better state park system, write to: California State Parks Foundtion, 900 Larkspur Landing Circle, Suite 175, P.O. Box 5668, Larkspur, CA 94939-5668. Or call (415) 461-2773.

San Diego area parks

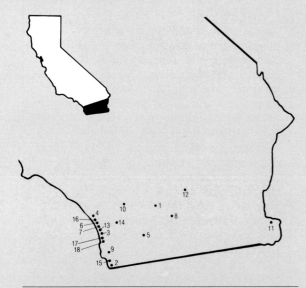

1 ANZA-BORREGO DESERT STATE PARK

Six hundred thousand acres of spectacular dunes, washes, wildflowers, palm groves, cacti, and dramatic sweeping vistas make this the largest state park in the continental United States. Look for roadrunners, golden eagles, kit foxes, mule deer, and bighorn sheep. Also iguanas, chuckwallas, and the red diamond rattlesnake. [Approximately 85 miles northeast of San Diego via I-8, Highways 79 and 78; 600,000 acres, 15'-6193' el. 173 developed sites; trailers 24', campers 31'. 52 sites with electricity, water, and sewer hookups for 31-foot vehicles. Unlimited primitive camping. Visitor Center. (616) 767-5311]

2 BORDER FIELD STATE PARK

Containing much of the Tijuana River estuary, this is an important wildlife habitat. Its salt and freshwater marshes give refuge to migratory waterfowl and resident wading birds such as black-necked stilt, avocet, teal, American widgeon, and pelican. It's also a good place for hiking, halibut fishing, and clam digging. [15 miles south of San Diego via I-5, Hollister and Monument roads; 680 acres, 0' el. (619) 428-3034]

3 CARDIFF STATE BEACH

Located on the San Diego Coast, which has been called the Riviera of the West, this gently sloping, sandy beach with pleasantly warm water offers swimming, sunning, surfing, and, best of all, relaxation. [1 mile south of Cardiff on Old Highway 101; 25 acres, 0' el. (619) 729-8947]

4 CARLSBAD STATE BEACH

Also located on the San Diego Coast, offering swimming, sunning, and surfing. [Carlsbad Blvd. at Tamarack in Carlsbad; 14 acres, 0' el. (619) 729-8947]

5 CUYAMACA RANCHO STATE PARK

Just east of San Diego; more than half the park is classified as "Wilderness," meaning all vehicles, even bicycles, are prohibited. Gorgeous pine and oak forests, broad meadows, spring-fed streams and more than 100 miles of riding and hiking trails. Recommended is the 3.5-mile Cuyamaca Peak Trail, which climbs to the 6,512-foot summit and a spectacular view of the Pacific Ocean, the Colorado Desert, Mexico, and the Salton Sea. [9 miles north of I-8 on Highway 79; 24,677 acres, 4132' el. 181 developed sites, trailers 27', campers 30'. Exhibits on Indians, gold mining, and natural history. (619) 765-0755]

6 LEUCADIA STATE BEACH

Another beach on the San Diego Coast. [Neptune at Fulvia in Leucadia; 11 acres, 0' el. (619) 729-8947]

7 MOONLIGHT STATE BEACH

Swimming, sunning, surfing, and relaxing are popular here. [West of I-5 on Encinitas Blvd. in Encinitas; 14 acres, 0' el. (619) 729-8947]

8 OCOTILLO WELLS STATE VEHICULAR RECREATION AREA

This park offers desert terrain for off-highway vehicles. The sights at dawn and dusk provide vistas of spectacular natural beauty. [Highway 78 at Ocotillo Wells; 14,532 acres, 100' el. Primitive camping, no water or restrooms. (619) 767-3545]

9 OLD TOWN SAN DIEGO STATE HISTORIC PARK

Step back in time and experience Californian life in the Mexican and early American periods. [San Diego Avenue and Twiggs Street, San Diego. 13 acres, 0' el. Restaurant and shop concessions. Open 10 a.m. to 6 p.m. in summer and 10 a.m. to 5 p.m. in winter. (619) 237-6770]

10 PALOMAR MOUNTAIN STATE PARK

Hike through the thick forest of pine, fir, and cedar trees that makes this one of the few southern California areas with a Sierra Nevada-like atmosphere. Just to the east of the park is the world-famous Palomar Observatory. Also, try the good trout fishing in Doane Pond. [From Escondido north on Highway S6, east 5 miles on Highway 76, north 9 miles on Highway S6, west on Highway S7 3 miles to park; 1,897 acres, 5161' el. 30 developed sites; trailers 21', campers 21'. (714) 742-3462]

11 PICACHO STATE RECREATION AREA

Offering gorgeous desert scenery along the lower Colorado River Basin, this area is popular for fishing, river-running, and desert exploration. In the area dominated by Picacho Peak, a plug-dome volcanic outcropping. Look for beavertail cactus, wild burros, bighorn sheep, and thousands of migratory waterfowl—Picacho is on one leg of the Pacific Flyway. [25 miles north of Winterhaven; 4,880 acres, 190' el. 50 primitive sites; trailers 24', campers 30'. No phone.]

12 SALTON SEA STATE RECREATION AREA

One of southern California's most popular boating parks, this is also one of the world's largest inland bodies of salt water. Fishing is excellent for orangemouth corvina, gulf croaker, and the perch-like sargo—all ocean transplants. [25 miles southeast of Indio on Highway 111; 17,900 acres, -220' el. 150 developed sites; trailers 30', campers 30'. 800 primitive sites. (619) 393-3052]

13 SAN ELIJO STATE BEACH

On the San Diego Coast, San Elijo offers swimming, sunning, and surfing. [On Old Highway 101 in Cardiff; 39 acres, 50' el. 171 developed sites; trailers 28', campers 30'. (619) 729-8947]

14 SAN PASQUAL BATTLEFIELD STATE HISTORIC PARK

This historical site commemorates the U.S. takeover of California. [8 miles south of Escondido on Highway 78; 11 acres, 400' el. Both General Stephen Kearny and Andres Pico claimed victory in a bloody engagement here between Dragoons and Californios. (619) 237-6768]

15 SILVER STRAND STATE BEACH

Named for the tiny silver seashells in the sand. Grunion spawn in the summer; beach combing is good for horn shells, moonsnails, cockleshells, and an occasional sand dollar. Lots of popular swimming and sunning areas. Keep an eye out for porpoises and the migrating gray whale. [4.5 miles south of Coronado on Highway 75; 428 acres 5' el. (619) 435-5184]

16 SOUTH CARLSBAD STATE BEACH

Another beautiful, easily accessible San Diego coastal beach. This sunny, sandy beach offers swimming, sunning, surfing, and simple relaxation (3 miles south of Carlsbad on Carlsbad Blvd., 135 acres, 50' el. 222 developed sites; trailers 28', campers 30'. (619) 729-8947

17 TORREY PINES STATE BEACH—

This beach can also be reached by trail from the reserve (see below). [1 mile south of Del Mar on North Torrey Pines Road; 41 acres, 0' el. (619) 755-2063]

18 TORREY PINES STATE RESERVE

This reserve features high broken cliffs and deep ravines on majestic headlands overlooking the sea. Its fragile environment is the home of the rare Torrey pine, a relic of the ice age. One designated natural preserve protects the trees, another protects Los Penasquitos Lagoon, one of the last salt marshes and waterfowl refuges in southern California. [1 mile south of Del Mar on North Torrey Pines road; 1,082 acres, 330' el. (619) 755-2063]

Park facilities and features

#	Park	Family campsites	Environmental campsites	Family & sites for hikers & bicyclists	Picnicking	Enroute campsites	Hiking trail	Fishing	Swimming	Boating	Horseback riding trails	Exhibits	Nature trail	Food services	Supplies	Trailer sanitation station	Designated underwater area
1	Anza-Borrego Desert State Park	★	•		★		•			•	★	•					
2	Border Field State Park				★		•	•	•		•		•				
3	Cardiff State Beach							•	•								
4	Carlsbad State Beach							•	•								
5	Cuyamaca Rancho State Park		•	★	★		•	•		•	★	•			•		
6	Leucadia State Beach							•	•								
7	Moonlight State Beach							•	•				★				
8	Ocotillo Wells State Vehicular Recreation Area	•															
9	Old Town San Diego State Historic Park				★						★	•	★				
10	Palomar Mountain State Park		★	★		•	★					•					
11	Picacho State Recreation Area	•		★		•	•		•		•			•			
12	Salton Sea State Recreation Area	★		★		★	•	★		★	•			•			
13	San Elijo State Beach		★				•	•					★				
14	San Pasqual Battlefield State Historic Park										•						
15	Silver Strand State Beach		★	•		•	★										
16	South Carlsbad State Beach		★			•	•						★	•			
17	Torrey Pines State Beach		★			•	•										
18	Torrey Pines State Reserve				★						★	★					

* *Not operated by State of California*
● *Features available*
★ *Features available and accessible to the physically disabled*

Telephone numbers are for area offices, staffed during regular business hours. The numbers for most parks are given in the listing; callers should be aware that many park offices are staffed only intermittently.

Coming attractions

These parks are currently under development. If you are interested in visiting one of them, check with the local district office of the Department of Parks and Recreation to find out if it's open to the public yet.

Burton Creek State Park (east of Tahoe State Recreation Area)

California Citrus Heritage State Historic Park (near Lake Elsinore)

John Little State Reserve (south of Julia Pfeiffer Burns State Park)

John Marsh State Historic Park (near Mount Diablo)

Lighthouse Field State Beach (next to Natural Bridges State Beach in Santa Cruz)

Olompali State Historic Park (south of Petaluma)

Reynolds Wayside Campground (south of Garberville near Smithe Redwoods State Reserve)

Santa Cruz Mission State Historic Park (in Santa Cruz)

Thornton State Beach (near Daly City)

Wilder Ranch State Park (near Santa Cruz)

In addition to the parks not operated by the state that are mentioned in the listings, these parks are also located on state-owned property but are under local jurisdiction. Except where otherwise indicated, they are operated by Los Angeles County: Baldwin Hills State Recreation Area, Dan Blocker State Beach, Otterbein State Recreation Area, Pan Pacific State Historic Park, Pyramid Lake (operated by the U.S. Forest Service), Seccombe Lake State Urban Recreation Area (operated by the City of San Bernardino), Watts Towers of Simon Rodia State Historic Park (operated by the City of Los Angeles), Willowbrook State Recreation Area, Woodland Opera House State Historic Park (operated by the City of Woodland).

Also available in the California Geographic Series . . .

California Mountain Ranges   by Russell B. Hill

Here is a book to match California's mountains. Thorough coverage of every range in the state combines with color photography that will take your breath away in Book One of the California Geographic Series. *California Mountain Ranges* will educate and enchant outdoor enthusiasts, mountaineers, and weekend travelers alike.

120 pages, 11" x 8½ ", $14.95 softcover, $24.95 hardcover

Coming Soon . . .

California Deserts   by Jerry Schad

Explore the remote vastness of the desert through the stunning color photography and authoritative text of *California Deserts*, Book Three in the California Geographic Series. Examine the fragile environment with its specially adapted plant and animal life, or just enjoy the cactus in bloom at Anza-Borrego. From resorts like Palm Springs to desolate places like the Old Woman Mountains, here is a portrait of this mysterious, brooding landscape, its history and its future.

120 pages, 11" x 8½", $14.95 softcover, $24.95 hardcover

To order:

California Mountain Ranges, California State Parks, **or** *California Deserts:*   Call toll free—1-800-582-BOOK—to order with Visa or Mastercard. Or send a check or money order and include $1.50 postage and handling for each book to Falcon Press, P.O. Box 279, Billings, MT 59103. [OUR GUARANTEE: If you are dissatisfied with any book obtained from Falcon Press, simply return your purchase for a full refund. All orders will be filled within three days upon receipt of the order.]